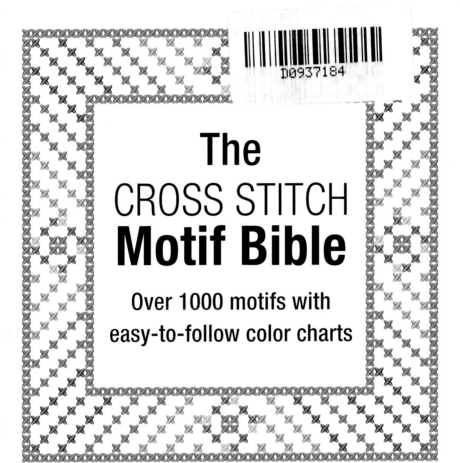

The
CROSS STITCH
Motif Bible

Over 1000 motifs with easy-to-follow color charts

JAN EATON
CHARTS BY CAROL AND JOHN WOODCOCK

kp books
An imprint of F+W Publications, Inc.
888-457-2873

kp books
An imprint of F+W Publications, Inc.
888-457-2873

A QUARTO BOOK

First published in North America in 2005
by KP Books
700 East State Street
Iola, WI 54990-0001

Library of Congress Catalog Card Number
20041133681
ISBN 0-89689-146-1

QUAR.CSBI

Conceived, designed, and produced by
Quarto Publishing plc
The Old Brewery
6 Blundell Street
London N7 9BH

Project editor Susie May
Senior art editor Penny Cobb
Designers Sheila Volpe, Carol Woodcock
Illustrators Coral Mula (pages 17–23),
    Carol and John Woodcock (pages 30–249)
Proofreader Tracie Davis
Indexer Geraldine Beare
Art director Moira Clinch
Publisher Paul Carslake

Color separation by Modern Age Repro House Ltd,
Hong Kong
Printed by Midas printing International Limited,
China

10 9 8 7 6 5 4 3 2 1

CONTENTS

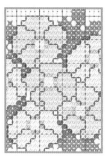

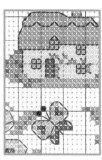

Flowers 30

Home and garden 50

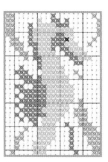

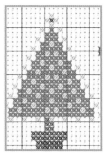

Natural world 68

Celebrations 88

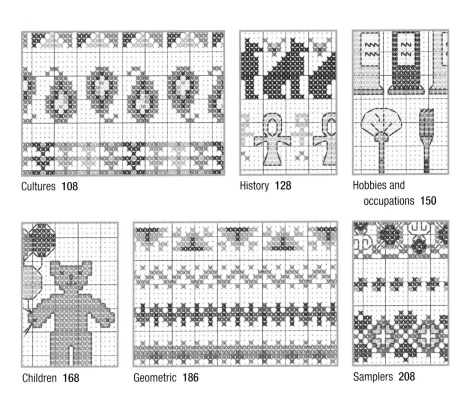

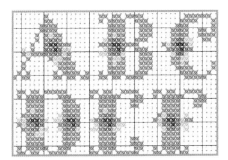

Introduction

Cross stitch is a very easy embroidery technique to work, and it quickly becomes addictive. To help you quench that addiction this book features over one thousand charted cross stitch designs, including alphabets, motifs, borders, and all-over patterns. The designs have been grouped together in the Pattern Library, which is split into separate sections for ease of use, however you can of course mix and match motifs and borders from any of the sections, and add lettering and numbers. *The Cross Stitch Motif Bible* gives the cross stitcher an almost limitless choice of combinations, so you can truly personalize your stitching.

Putting it all together

There are many ways that you can use the charts in this book to create unique, individual works of embroidery. You can pick out preferred motifs, styles of lettering, and borders and put them all together using the guidelines in Design Tips (*see page 23*). You can use the colors I have suggested or put together your own combinations. Finally, you can make your works of embroidery into any number of different finished items.

The palette of 58 colors used for the charts is based on the DMC floss range. A list of actual code numbers and color names is provided on page 254, accompanied by their nearest Anchor floss equivalents. Please feel free to experiment with your own color combinations, adding specialty threads, metallic threads, and beads to create the exact effect to suit you.

◊ **WEDDING HEARTS**
TOM PUDDING DESIGNS
Flowers, bold initials, and a large heart motif combine to make a simple yet effective sampler to commemorate a wedding.

◊ SMALL MOTIF SAMPLER
Tom Pudding Designs
A selection of traditional
sampler motifs are
contained within a narrow
border to make this
pleasing arrangement.
Tiny silver-colored metal
charms are added
to the design.

Many cross stitchers choose white, cream, or ecru fabric as the background for their stitching, and pale, neutral shades show off the thread colors well, but don't forget that there is a wide variety of other color choices that you can explore. Bright, hot colors can make a simple design look very up-to-the-minute, and dark colors show off an intricately stitched pattern to great effect.

You can also be adventurous when turning your pieces of cross stitch into finished items. Traditional framed samplers are undoubtedly beautiful, as are cross-stitch decorated pillowcases, but perhaps you would prefer to use your embroidery in a whole new way. You could try: stitching a selection of brightly colored fruit motifs (see pages 58–63) on coarse evenweave linen and mounting it in a sleek modern frame to display in a dining area; repeating rows of tiny motifs, such as the smaller butterflies on pages 73–75, on lengths of Aida or linen band and sewing them onto table and bed linen; or mounting your stitching in a box lid or on the front of a simple fabric bag. Even tiny pieces of cross stitch can look lovely made into a pincushion, scissors keeper, or perfumed lavender bag.

Whatever you decide, I hope you enjoy choosing and stitching the designs in the book and that you are ultimately delighted with the finished results.

8

How to use this book

The first section of this book takes you through the materials and techniques needed for working cross stitch embroidery, before moving on to the Pattern Library, which contains over 1,000 motifs for cross stitch with integral color keys. Motif sizes and thread details are then given at the end of the library.

From choosing fabric and threads to working the stitches, each technique is explained in easy-to-follow steps.

The techniques are accompanied by step-by-step photographs and illustrations.

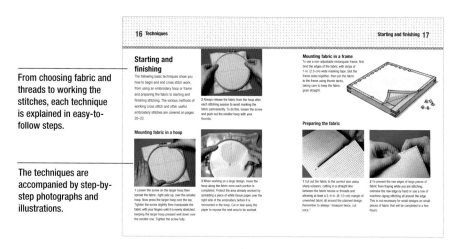

Starting and finishing

The following basic techniques show you how to begin and end cross stitch work, from using an embroidery hoop or frame and preparing the fabric to starting and finishing stitching. The various methods of working cross stitch and other useful embroidery stitches are covered on pages 20–22.

Mounting fabric in a hoop

1 Loosen the screw on the larger hoop then spread the fabric, right side up, over the smaller hoop. Now press the larger hoop over the top. Tighten the screw slightly then manipulate the fabric with your fingers until it is evenly stretched, keeping the larger hoop pressed well down over the smaller one. Tighten the screw fully.

2 Always release the fabric from the hoop after each stitching session to avoid marking the fabric permanently. To do this, loosen the screw and push out the smaller hoop with your thumbs.

3 When working on a large design, move the hoop along the fabric once each portion is completed. Protect the area already worked by spreading a piece of white tissue paper over the right side of the embroidery before it is remounted in the hoop. Cut or tear away the paper to expose the next area to be worked.

Mounting fabric in a frame

To use a non-adjustable rectangular frame, first bind the edges of the fabric with strips of 1-in. (2.5-cm) wide masking tape. Slot the frame sides together, then pin the fabric to the frame using thumb tacks, taking care to keep the fabric grain straight.

Preparing the fabric

1 Cut out the fabric to the correct size using sharp scissors, cutting in a straight line between the fabric blocks or threads and allowing at least a 3–4-in. (8–10-cm) margin of unworked fabric all around the planned design. Remember to always 'measure twice, cut once.'

2 To prevent the raw edges of large pieces of fabric from fraying while you are stitching, oversew the raw edge by hand or use a row of machine /zigzag stitching all around the edge. This is not necessary for small designs on small pieces of fabric that will be completed in a few hours.

READING A CHART

A cross stitch design is worked from a chart onto evenweave fabric by counting the blocks or threads in the fabric to position the stitches accurately. Each cross stitch is represented in this book by a colored cross occupying one block of fabric. Unfilled fabric blocks on a motif, letter, or border show the number of unworked blocks that separate groups of stitches. As a general rule, start stitching at the center of a cross stitch design, working outward from the center of the chart by working one complete cross stitch for every colored cross shown on the chart.

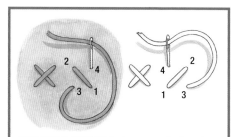

FORMING THE STITCHES Each cross can be formed exactly as shown above left, or the top and bottom diagonal stitches can be worked to slant in the opposite direction as shown above right. Whichever way you prefer to stitch, remember to be consistent, making sure the top diagonals of each cross slant in the same direction.

CATEGORY The motifs are divided into 11 different themes.

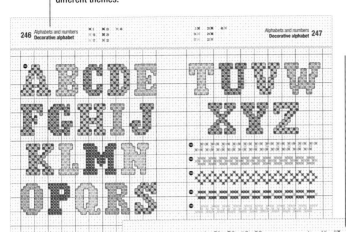

STITCH COLOR KEY A key runs across the top of each page and indicates which thread color should be used to stitch each cross shown on the chart. Fifty-eight colors are used throughout the book and each color is cross-referenced to both DMC and Anchor floss manufacturer numbers on page 254.

NUMBERS Each motif is numbered and cross-referenced to the list of motif sizes at the back of the book.

BACKGROUND GRID To make counting easier, the background grid on each page is divided by thin black lines into blocks of five squares by five.

BACKSTITCH LINES are used to outline and define areas of cross stitch and these are shown as straight stitches on the charts.

FRENCH KNOTS are tiny, raised stitches that add detail and are often used to depict an eye on a bird or animal. They are shown on the charts as tiny solid dots.

What you will need

Cross stitch does not demand an expensive initial outlay to get you started. Fabric, thread, needles, and an embroidery hoop are all you need to begin stitching. You will then find that as you collect unused fabric and extra threads you can build up a useful embroidery kit for future projects.

Fabric

There are two main varieties of fabric used for cross stitch work, referred to as evenweave and Aida fabrics, although Aida is still evenly woven. Either of these evenweave fabrics make a good choice for cross stitch because the evenly woven warp and weft threads allow the cross stitches to be made of identical size and to be positioned accurately on the fabric.

Evenweave fabric Evenweave fabric has the same number of warp and weft threads woven to every 1 in. (2.5cm) of fabric. The number of threads is called the count and this number varies depending on the weight of the individual threads. The most popular sizes are 28- and 36-count, which contain 28 or 36 threads to every 1 in. (2.5cm). Cross stitch is usually worked over pairs of evenweave threads rather than single threads, which means that when you stitch on 28-count evenweave you can fit 14 stitches into 1 in. (2.5cm) of fabric.

Evenweave fabric can be made from linen, cotton, or a blend that may contain synthetic fibers such as polyester.

Aida fabric The most popular evenly woven cotton fabric for cross stitch is called Aida, and varies in appearance to the traditional evenweave fabric described above. For Aida, groups of even-sized threads are woven together to produce a series of distinct blocks, over which individual stitches are worked. The blocks are easy to count accurately so this fabric is perfect for a beginner. Like traditional evenweave, Aida is available in different counts: 14-count Aida—14 blocks to 1 in. (2.5cm)—is one of the most widely used sizes, allowing you to fit 14 stitches to every 1 in. (2.5cm) of fabric; 11-count Aida—11 blocks to 1 in. (2.5cm)—has a larger weave so stitches are bigger, while stitches worked on 16- or 18-count are smaller.

◊ LEFT TO RIGHT
26-count evenweave linen, 26-count evenweave cotton, and 32-count evenweave linen.

◊ TOP TO BOTTOM
18-count cream Aida, 14-count beige Aida, 14-count pink Aida, and 14-count cream Aida with lurex.

Cross stitch bands Narrow bands of fabric made specifically for cross stitch are available by the yard or meter in various widths. They are useful for trimming items of home furnishing as well as for making small items such as bookmarks and scented sachets. The central portion of the bands is made from either evenweave linen or Aida and the top and bottom edges are prefinished with a decorative edging. The bands can be bought in several colors and they are usually woven with 14 blocks or 28 threads to every 1 in. (2.5cm).

Fabric counts Two strawberries (motif 149, page 58) have been stitched in cotton floss on different counts of cross stitch fabric.

⬭ SAMPLE 1 was stitched on 11-count Aida fabric using three strands of floss for the cross stitches and two strands for the backstitch outlines.

Threads

Stranded cotton floss is most commonly used for cross stitch, but silk, rayon, specialty, or metallic threads can also be experimented with for varying effects.

Cotton floss Cotton floss is the most versatile thread to use for cross stitch. It is available in a wide range of colors and consists of six loosely twisted strands of mercerized cotton. A cut length of floss can be split into different weights to suit different fabric counts. As a general rule, use two strands for stitching on 14-count Aida fabric or over two threads on 28-count evenweave fabric, and three strands for stitching on 11-count Aida fabric. Use floss in 15–18-in. (38–45-cm) lengths to avoid tangling.

⬭ SAMPLE 2 was stitched on 14-count Aida fabric using two strands of floss for the cross stitches and one strand for the backstitch outlines.

⬭ SAMPLE 3 was stitched over two threads of 28-count evenweave linen using two strands of floss for the cross stitches and one strand for the backstitch outlines.

⬭ SAMPLE 4 was stitched on 16-count Aida using two strands of floss for the cross stitches and one strand for the backstitch outlines.

Tip

When using specialty threads the colors will blend and flow better if you work your cross stitches individually, rather than in rows. In this example individual cross stitches (top block) achieve a clearer effect when using an over-dyed floss than stitches worked in horizontal rows (bottom block).

If you don't want to buy a specialty thread, another way of creating an unusual color effect is to thread a strand of two or more contrasting or toning solid-colored floss threads in the needle at the same time. This is known as blending or tweeding, and looks very effective when stitching natural forms such as flowers and foliage.

Rayon and silk floss Floss is also made from rayon or pure silk. Both types are slightly more expensive but they have a delightful sheen and the colors are vibrant. When using rayon or silk floss, cut a shorter length than usual and choose a tapestry needle with a large enough eye to accommodate the thread comfortably, otherwise it will rub and fray each time you pull the needle through the fabric. Take care to finish off the thread ends carefully when stitching with rayon thread, which is fairly springy.

Specialty threads Over-dyed and hand-painted floss, often known as specialty threads, offer a wide range of color mixtures and effects, depending on the manufacturer. Several different shades or colors are applied to the thread at fixed intervals so that they blend into each other. These threads are more expensive than cotton floss in solid colors so should be used in small amounts to add an extra special dash of color to a design.

Metallic threads Like specialty threads (*left*) metallic threads can be used to add accents of color and sparkle to a design. They are available in metallic, pearlized, and fluorescent finishes and in varying weights, so choose one

> **Tip**
> For just a hint of sparkle, combine a length of blending filament—a very fine metallic thread—with solid cotton floss in the needle.

to suit the count of fabric you are using. Fine braid No. 4 works well on 14-count Aida and 28-count evenweave fabric.

Needles

Tapestry needles are ideal for use with all evenweave fabrics because their blunt points slide easily through the material without pulling or tearing. These needles are available in different sizes, graded from thick—the low numbers—to fine—the high numbers. The most useful sizes for cross stitch are 24, 26, and 28.

Hoops and frames

For all but the smallest designs, mounting the fabric in a circular hoop or rectangular frame will help you to stitch evenly and accurately.

Embroidery hoops are available in various sizes and consist of two circular sections placed one inside the other. The fabric is sandwiched between the two sections and secured by a screw at the side. The advantage of using a hoop is that it can be moved across the fabric once each portion of the design has been completed.

Rectangular frames consist of straight wooden bars that slot together and, like hoops,

are available in a good range of sizes. The fabric is attached to the frame using thumb tacks. Unlike a hoop, a frame cannot be moved across the fabric so choose one to suit the size of your work, ensuring that unsightly tack marks do not run into the finished piece.

Graph paper and design materials

Graph paper is an essential design tool, along with a pen, scissors, and ruler. Using this basic equipment you can choose any number of motifs and combine and space them to create a pleasing arrangement.

Beads

To add interest to a stitched design you can substitute glass seed beads for some of the cross stitches. Size 11 seed beads fit the weave of 14-count Aida or 28-count evenweave fabric perfectly, so you can apply one bead to one Aida block or pair of evenweave threads. Use a special beading needle or the finest gauge of crewel needle (size 10) to work the stitches when applying beads and match the thread color to the fabric background, not to the color of the bead.

◊ USING BEADS Green and gold seed beads have been used for the foliage and pips instead of green and yellow cross stitches on these two strawberries (motif 149, page 58) stitched on 14-count Aida using two strands of cotton floss.

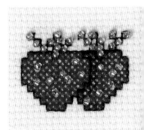

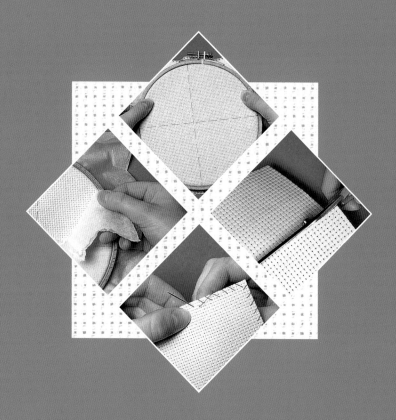

Chapter

Techniques

In this chapter, you will find a wealth of expert information to help you start cross stitching, choose fabric and threads, and look after your work. There are also helpful hints on how to use and combine the motifs from the Pattern Library to create your own cross stitch designs.

Starting and finishing

The following basic techniques show you how to begin and end cross stitch work, from using an embroidery hoop or frame and preparing the fabric to starting and finishing stitching. The various methods of working cross stitch and other useful embroidery stitches are covered on pages 20–22.

2 Always release the fabric from the hoop after each stitching session to avoid marking the fabric permanently. To do this, loosen the screw and push out the smaller hoop with your thumbs.

Mounting fabric in a hoop

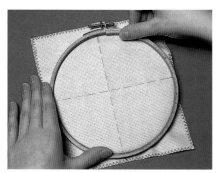

1 Loosen the screw on the larger hoop then spread the fabric, right side up, over the smaller hoop. Now press the larger hoop over the top. Tighten the screw slightly then manipulate the fabric with your fingers until it is evenly stretched, keeping the larger hoop pressed well down over the smaller one. Tighten the screw fully.

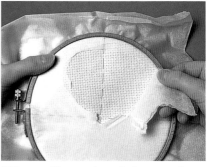

3 When working on a large design, move the hoop along the fabric once each portion is completed. Protect the area already worked by spreading a piece of white tissue paper over the right side of the embroidery before it is remounted in the hoop. Cut or tear away the paper to expose the next area to be worked.

Mounting fabric in a frame

To use a non-adjustable rectangular frame, first bind the edges of the fabric with strips of 1-in. (2.5-cm) wide masking tape. Slot the frame sides together, then pin the fabric to the frame using thumb tacks, taking care to keep the fabric grain straight.

Preparing the fabric

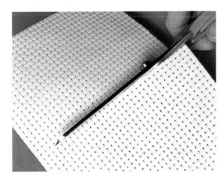

1 Cut out the fabric to the correct size using sharp scissors, cutting in a straight line between the fabric blocks or threads and allowing at least a 3–4-in. (8–10-cm) margin of unworked fabric all around the planned design. Remember to always "measure twice, cut once."

2 To prevent the raw edges of large pieces of fabric from fraying while you are stitching, oversew the raw edge by hand or use a row of machine zigzag stitching all around the edge. This is not necessary for small designs on small pieces of fabric that will be completed in a few hours.

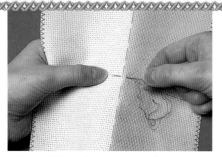

3 Cross stitch is always worked outward from the center of the design, to ensure there is an even margin of fabric all around the finished piece. To find the center, fold the fabric into quarters and mark the point where the folds join with a pin. Unfold the fabric and work two rows of basting stitches along the folds so the rows cross at this point. Use a contrasting color of sewing thread for the basting so that the stitches are easy to see. Starting at the center of the fabric, work the group of stitches nearest to the center of the chart. Work the remainder of the design outward from these stitches by counting the squares on the chart to determine the placing of the stitches.

Starting to stitch

There are several ways to anchor the thread end when you begin stitching, so choose the method that feels most comfortable to you.

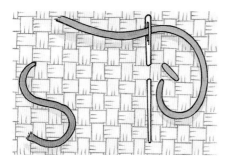

Loose-end start Take the needle through to the wrong side of the fabric close to where you intend to start stitching and leave a 2-in. (5-cm) length of thread hanging loose on the surface. Continue stitching until you finish the length of thread (*see* Finishing off the thread, *right*), then return to the loose end, take it through to the wrong side and darn it in under a group of stitches.

Waste-knot start Tie a knot at the end of the thread. Take the needle through to the wrong side of the fabric a short distance away from where you will be stitching, so the thread on the back lies along the position of the first few stitches. Work the stitches up to the knot, securing the thread on the back, then carefully snip off the knot.

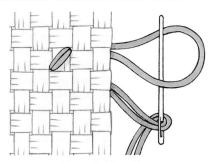

Loop start When stitching with an even number of strands of thread you can use the

loop start. Cut the thread twice as long as usual. To loop start when using two strands, simply fold the thread in half and thread the cut ends through the eye of the needle, making a loop at the other end. Bring the needle through the fabric at the beginning of the first stitch and pull the thread through to leave the loop on the wrong side. Make the first stitch, take the needle to the wrong side, slip it through the loop and pull gently to anchor the end.

Finishing off the thread

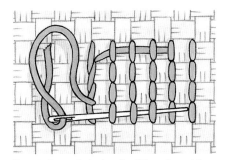

Close to the end of a length of thread, or at the end of a design element, take the needle through to the wrong side of the fabric. Slide the needle through the last few stitches you have worked, pull gently and cut off the thread end. Don't be tempted to carry a length of thread across the wrong side between two stitched areas because this may show through on the right side and spoil the stitching. Instead, fasten off the thread after each area is completed.

Joining in a new length

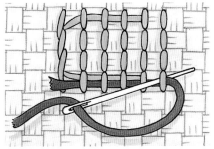

On the wrong side of the fabric, take the new length of thread under the back of several stitches close to where you are stitching. Take a small stitch over the last stitch already worked and bring the needle through the fabric ready to begin stitching.

The stitches

Cross stitches can be worked individually or in rows. Individual stitches should be used for small areas of color, while rows of stitches are suitable for filling in solid blocks of color. Backstitch and French knots are the other stitches used with cross stitch, to make straight lines or solid dots for eyes, and the stitch for applying beads can also be useful to learn.

Individual cross stitch

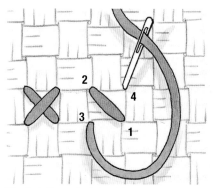

The first diagonal stitch of the cross slants from bottom right to top left. Bring the needle through at 1 and insert it at 2 to make a half-cross stitch. Complete the cross by stitching the second diagonal from bottom left (3) to top right (4). Repeat as required.

Cross stitch in horizontal rows

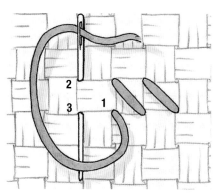

1 Each row of crosses is worked over two horizontal journeys. On the first journey, work from right to left making a row of evenly spaced diagonal stitches. Bring the needle through at 1 and insert it at 2. Bring the needle through at 3, ready to make the next stitch at the left. Repeat as required along the row.

2 At the end of the row, turn and work back in the opposite direction making diagonal stitches to complete the crosses. Insert the needle at 4 and bring it through at 5. Work the next and subsequent rows below the first and repeat until the block of color is completed.

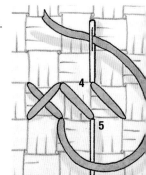

Cross stitch in vertical rows

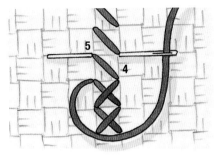

1 Each row of crosses is worked over two vertical journeys. On the first journey, work from top to bottom making a row of evenly spaced diagonal stitches. Bring the needle through at 1 and insert it at 2. Bring the needle through at 3, ready to make the next stitch below. Repeat as required along the row.

2 At the end of the row, work back in the opposite direction making diagonal stitches to complete the crosses. Insert the needle at 4 and bring it through at 5. Work the next and subsequent rows at the left of the first and repeat until the block of color is completed.

Backstitch

Work backstitch from right to left, making straight stitches forward and backward along the row. Bring the needle through at 1 and insert it to the right at 2, then bring it through again at 3. To make the next stitch, insert the needle at the left-hand end of the previous stitch. Backstitches may be vertical, horizontal, or diagonal and cover one or more fabric blocks.

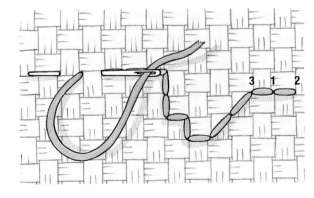

French knots

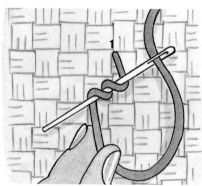

1 Bring the needle through at 1. Holding the thread taut with your left hand, twist the needle around the thread several times and gently tighten the twists.

2 Holding the thread taut, turn the needle and insert it a short distance away at 2. Keeping the thread taut, take the needle through to the back, forming a knot at 2.

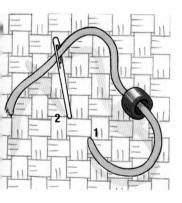

Applying beads

Attach each bead with a half-cross stitch. Bring the needle through at 1, thread the bead, and insert the needle at 2. For a more secure fixing, make a second diagonal stitch through the bead in the same way.

Beading tips

- Choose a suitable bead size to match the count of your fabric.
- Take care to fasten off thread ends securely to avoid the beads becoming loose and pulling away from the fabric.
- Match the thread color to that of the fabric, not the bead.
- Some highly colored beads are not colorfast, so wash and press your embroidery before applying them.

Design tips

Here are some useful guidelines for combining multiple motifs, alphabets, and borders to design samplers and pictures.

Adding corners to a border

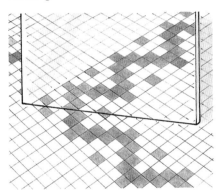

There are plenty of borders in the book that can be used just as they are, but you will probably also want to use a border pattern to make a continuous frame around a sampler, or to edge a tablecloth or decorative runner. To help you work out a good corner design from your chosen border, first draw a length of the border on graph paper and color it in. Angle a small mirror at 45 degrees to the drawn border then move the mirror until you achieve a satisfactory corner arrangement—made by the drawn border and the reflected image. Now draw the arrangement in on the graph paper.

Combining motifs to make a sampler

To build up the design for a sampler using several motifs from the book, start by drawing your chosen motifs on graph paper. If you plan to repeat the same motif draw it out as many times as required. Cut out each graph-paper

◁ MY FAVORITE SAMPLER
TOM PUDDING DESIGNS
This large, elaborate sampler combines many pictorial and geometric motifs arranged round a central alphabet. A wide range of thread colors have been used, together with tiny seed beads and a gilt charm.

◊ RED ALPHABETS
TOM PUDDING DESIGNS
A simple arrangement of alphabets
stitched in shades of red thread on white
fabric works well surrounded by an
antique wooden cross frame.

motif leaving a margin of one or two squares all
around each one. Now spread the motifs out on
a large sheet of graph paper and begin moving
them around until you are happy with the
arrangement, adding lettering if you wish. When
using lots of small motifs try arranging them in
neat rows, as if you were placing them on a
chessboard. When you are happy with the
arrangement stick each motif in position using
double-sided tape.

Spacing letters and numbers

As well as personalizing your own stitching by
adding your name and the date of completion,
you may also want to add lettering to special
gifts, such as a wedding or other
commemorative sampler. Write out the words
you would like to use and choose one of the
alphabets from the book. The height of each
alphabet is given on page 253. For example, 7h
means that each letter is seven crosses high
when stitched. Use the same technique of
drawing each letter or number on graph paper
as if you were making a sampler (*see above*).
Cut out the letters, leaving a one-square margin
all around, then arrange them to form words. As
a general guideline, space all the letters or
numbers out evenly, remembering that you will
need to leave a larger gap between words than
you do between individual letters. For a small

alphabet, try leaving a space of a single square
between letters and two squares between
words. When you are happy with the spacing,
double check the spelling before sticking each
letter in place with double-sided tape.

Making a key

Choose a selection of threads to stitch your
design with and then color in the different
motifs using fiber-tip pens or colored pencils in
similar colors to the threads. For every color
you use, draw and fill in a small square along
the side of the chart to make a key. Write the
code number of each thread by the relevant
colored-in square.

Working guidelines

Following a few simple guidelines can help you work with ease, and ensure that your embroidery stays looking fresh. Using good quality fabric and threads and taking care over your work will make the difference between a standard piece of cross stitch embroidery and a future heirloom.

• **The best you can afford** Choose the best quality fabric and threads you can afford so that your cross stitch projects will look great, and stay that way for many years.

• **Buy more than you need** When buying fabric for a project, particularly an expensive evenweave linen, don't believe you are being economical by buying exactly the amount you need to fit your design. It is far better to buy a slightly larger piece of fabric that you can trim down once the stitching is complete—if you miscalculate and the edge of the stitching finishes up too close to the fabric edge, you may not be able to use it.

• **Basting guidelines** If you are not a very experienced stitcher it can help to baste a grid of running stitches across the fabric before you begin cross stitching. On Aida fabric work rows of running stitches ten blocks apart and on evenweave fabric work them twenty threads apart. This divides the fabric into ten-stitch blocks that make following a chart easier.

• **Work outward** Start stitching at the center of the design and work outward so that you have an even margin of fabric all around the stitched design.

• **Work cleanly** Nothing spoils a piece of cross stitch more than grubby fingerprints or a dirty ring where the fabric has been rubbed around an embroidery hoop. Always wash your hands thoroughly before starting to stitch and at regular intervals during your stitching session, and avoid using hand cream when you are stitching because the oils in the cream may transfer to the fabric. It is also good practice to take an embroidery out of its hoop at the end of each stitching session.

• **Avoid fluff** Try to avoid wearing dark-colored garments that shed while you are stitching—angora or mohair jumpers are the worst because the tiny hairs they shed get trapped beneath the stitches. If fluff accumulates on your work clean it off by wrapping adhesive tape around your hand, sticky side out, and gently dabbing it over the surface of the stitching.

• **Care for work in progress** Store threads and unfinished work in a clean, dark, and dry place. An old, well-washed cotton pillowcase is ideal for this, but if you decide to use a paper bag or embroidery tote bag for temporary storage, protect your work from dirt by wrapping it in white, acid-free tissue paper first. Store leftover threads carefully. You can buy precut card bobbins to wind the threads round, or cut out your own from a sheet of thin card. Make a note of the brand and color number of the thread on each card, place the cards in a dustproof box, then store in a cool, dry place.

Looking after your completed work

When your stitching is complete, give some thought to how best to look after it, so that you and your family can enjoy the fruits of your labor for many years to come.

Washing guidelines

Make it a cast-iron rule to treat spills and stains as soon as they occur and mend tears or holes before laundering. If you are worried that the threads used in a piece may not be colorfast, have the item dry cleaned.

Embroidered items such as table linen and pillowcases that are intended to be used rather than displayed will need to be laundered. The best way to do this is to wash the items carefully by hand in hand-hot water with a mild, detergent-free cleaning agent. Most specialist fabric shampoos are ideal, but check that the one you choose does not contain optical brighteners, which will cause colors to fade.

Rinse the piece thoroughly in several changes of water, then roll it in a towel and press gently to remove surplus water. Gently ease the embroidery into shape and leave to dry out of direct sunlight.

Pressing guidelines

Press embroidered pieces while they are still slightly damp. Pad the ironing surface with a couple of old, clean towels then lay the embroidery over them with the wrong side uppermost. Cover with a piece of clean white fabric—an old cotton sheet is perfect. Set the iron to a temperature that matches the

composition of the fabric: linen setting for evenweave linen; slightly cooler for Aida and cotton fabrics; and a lower synthetic setting for fabric made from a cotton/synthetic blend. Press lightly, taking care not to flatten the stitches.

Storage

Frame pictures to eliminate dust and dirt and store items such as table and bed linen carefully when not in use.

The main enemies that can attack embroideries, apart from dust and dirt, are direct sunlight and strong artificial lighting, which cause colors to fade and fibers to weaken. Heat makes both the threads and fabric brittle, while damp rots the fibers, so display framed pieces carefully, avoiding positions close to fireplaces and radiators and rooms with humid atmospheres, such as bathrooms.

Try not to store fabric items for any length of time in polythene bags because the polythene

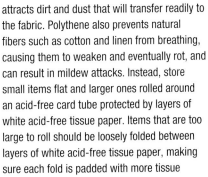

attracts dirt and dust that will transfer readily to the fabric. Polythene also prevents natural fibers such as cotton and linen from breathing, causing them to weaken and eventually rot, and can result in mildew attacks. Instead, store small items flat and larger ones rolled around an acid-free card tube protected by layers of white acid-free tissue paper. Items that are too large to roll should be loosely folded between layers of white acid-free tissue paper, making sure each fold is padded with more tissue paper. Store all the items in their own, clean, fabric bag in a drawer, cupboard, or other dark, dry, and moth-free place.

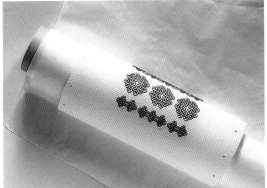

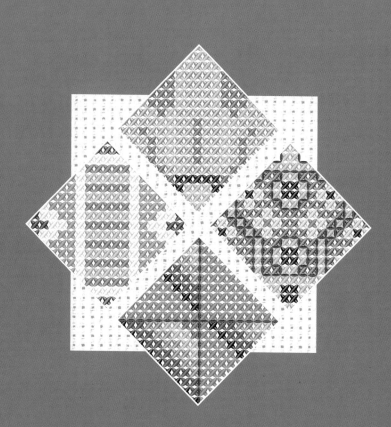

Chapter

Pattern Library

The Pattern Library contains charts for over 1000 cross stitch motifs, divided into eleven different themes for ease of use. Each page is accompanied by a key showing the colors used. Details of motif sizes and thread numbers are given at the end of the library.

30 Flowers
Roses 1

⊠ 1   ⊠ 16   ⊠ 45   ⊠ 54
⊠ 11 ⊠ 17   ⊠ 46   ⊠ 56
⊠ 15 ⊠ 18   ⊠ 53

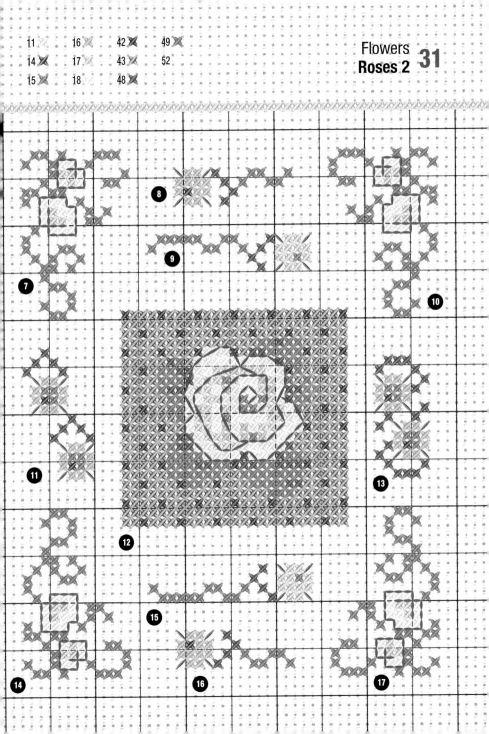

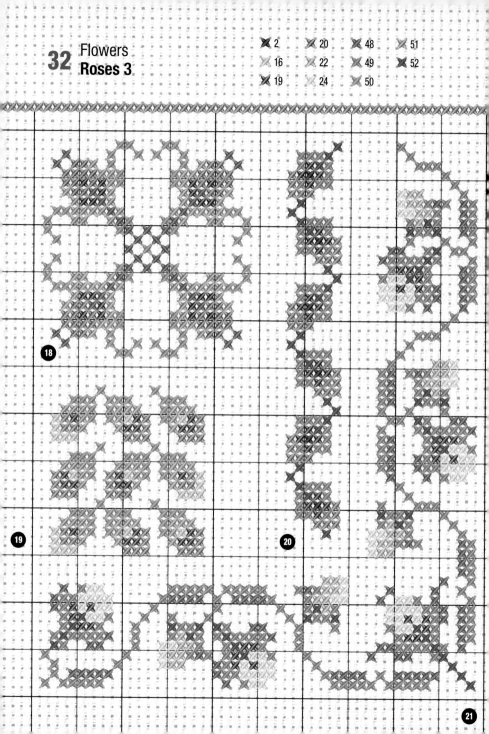

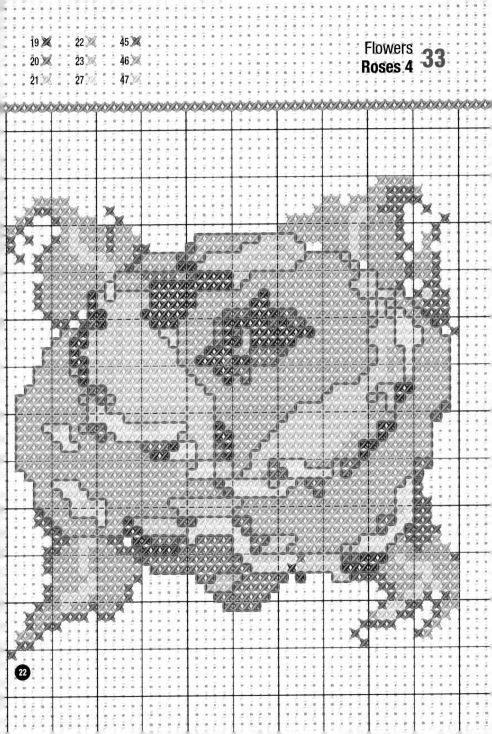

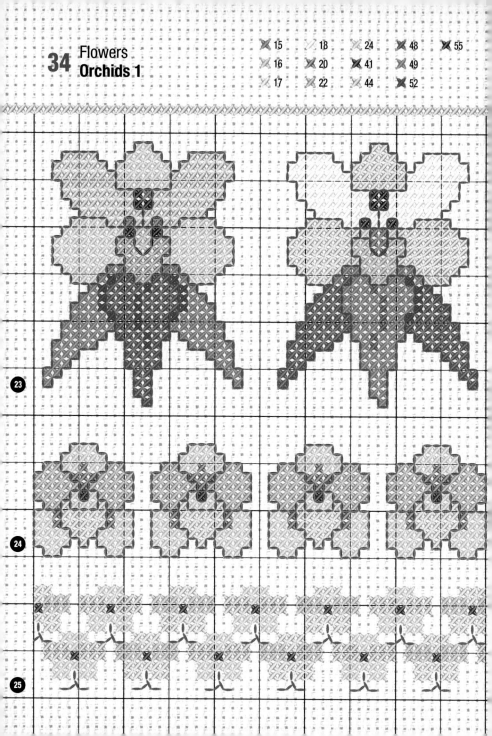

34 Flowers
Orchids 1

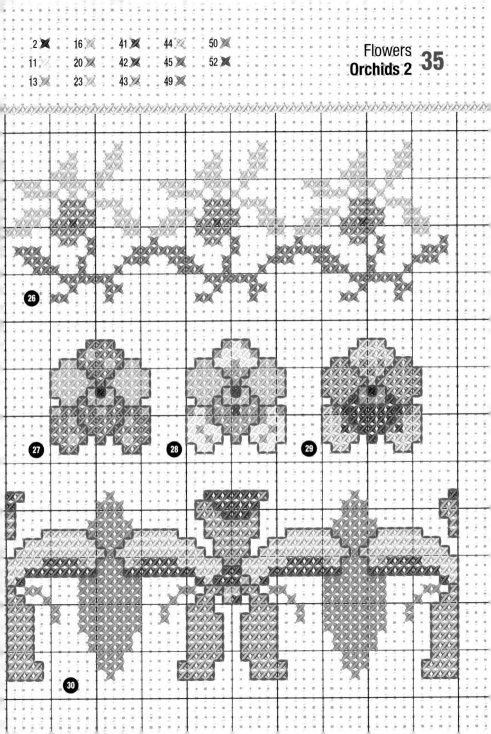

36 Flowers
Tulips 1

✕ 16	✕ 19	✕ 32	✕ 49
✕ 17	✕ 20	✕ 33	✕ 50
✕ 18	✕ 31	✕ 45	

17 23 49
20 45 50
22 46

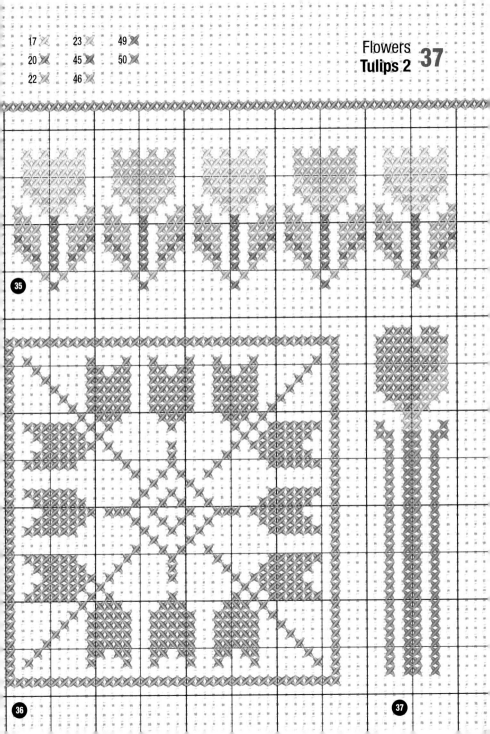

35

36 37

38 Flowers
Flowers and bows 1

✖ 2 ✖ 16 ✖ 31 ✖ 38
✖ 8 ✖ 19 ✖ 32 ✖ 45
✖ 15 ✖ 30 ✖ 37 ✖ 53

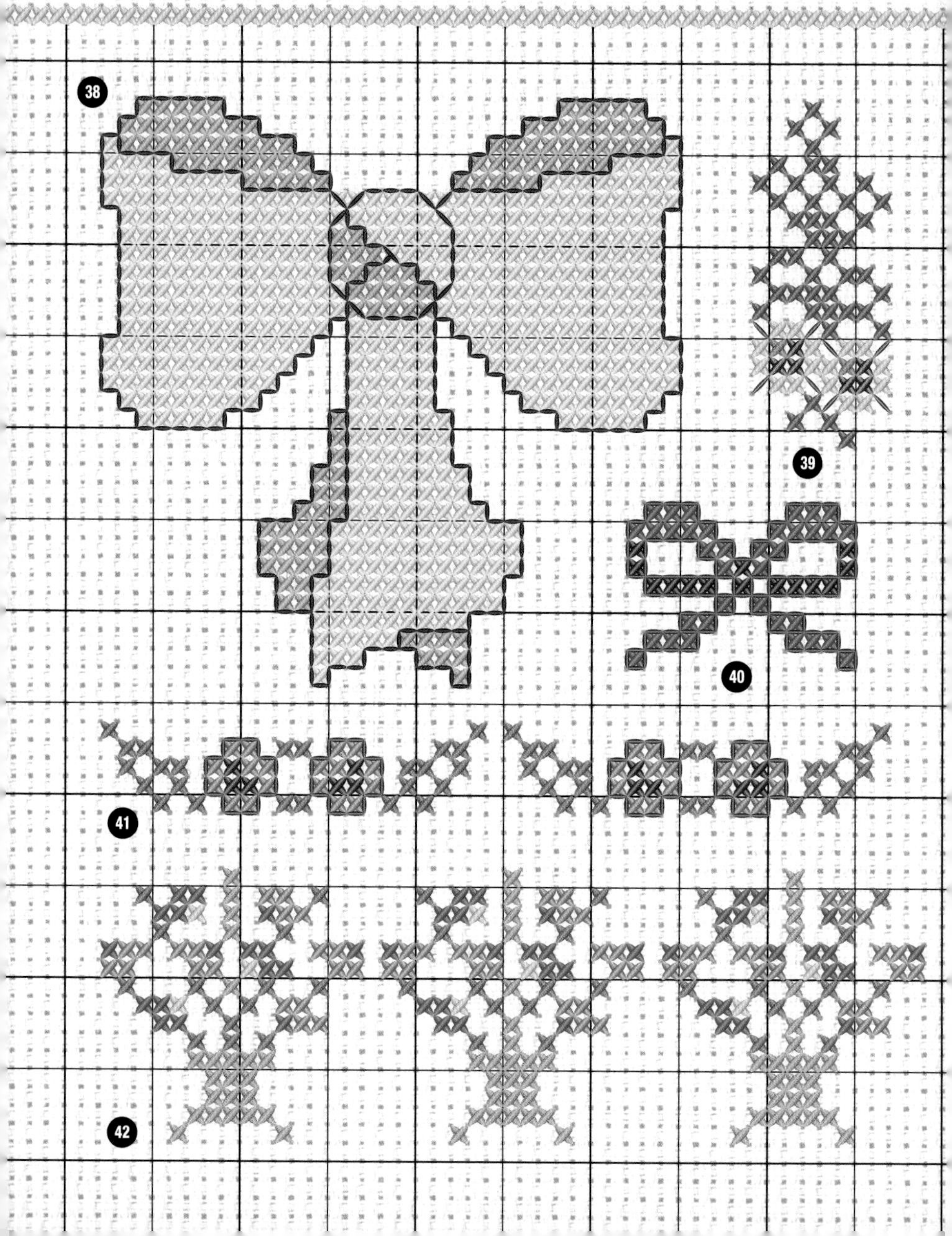

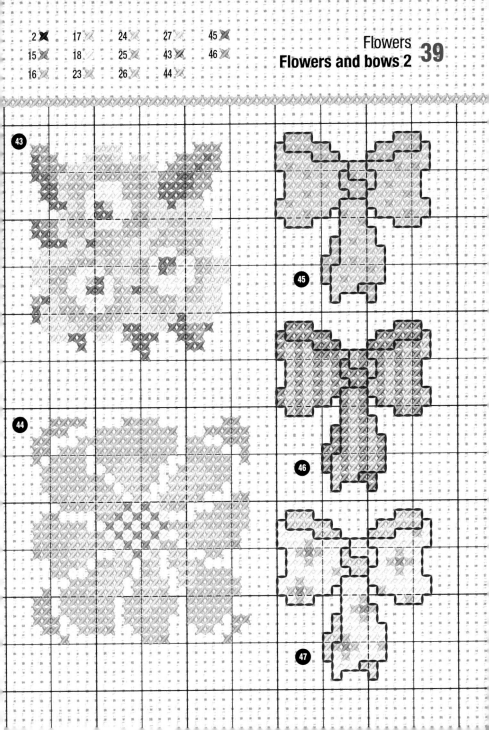

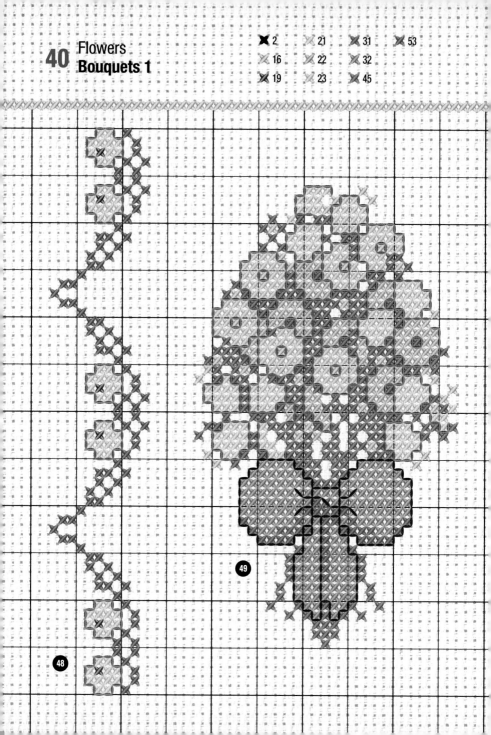

40 Flowers Bouquets 1

✕ 2   ✕ 21   ✕ 31   ✕ 53
✕ 16   ✕ 22   ✕ 32
✕ 19   ✕ 23   ✕ 45

2 ✖ 41 ✖ 44 ✖
16 ✖ 42 ✖ 49 ✖
17 ✖ 43 ✖ 55 ✖

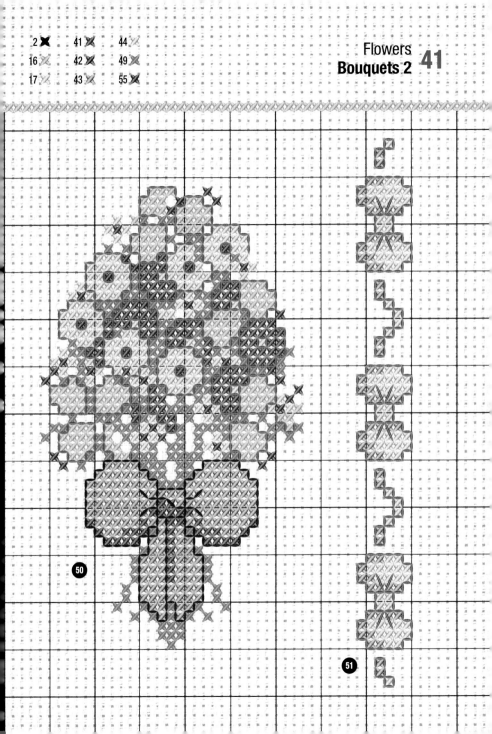

Flowers

42 Flower motifs 1

✕ 14	✕ 17	✕ 49
✕ 15	✕ 45	✕ 52
✕ 16	✕ 46	✕ 55

52

53   54   55

2 ✖ 15 ✖ 18 55 ✖
6 ✖ 16 ✖ 19 ✖
14 ✖ 17 ✖ 20 ✖

1	✕ 19	27	✕ 51
✕ 15	✕ 25	✕ 49	
18	26	✕ 50	

59

60

61

16　　26　　49　　56

19　　37　　50　　57

25　　40　　52

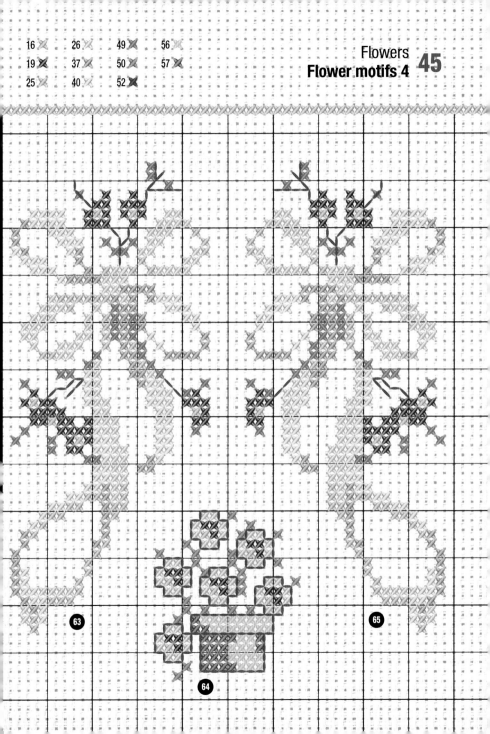

46 Flowers
Flower borders 1

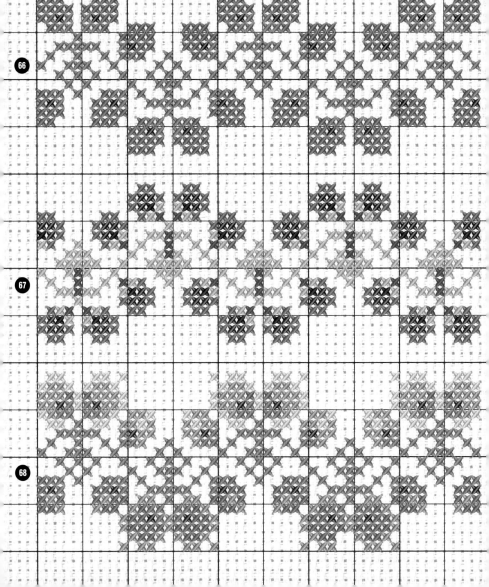

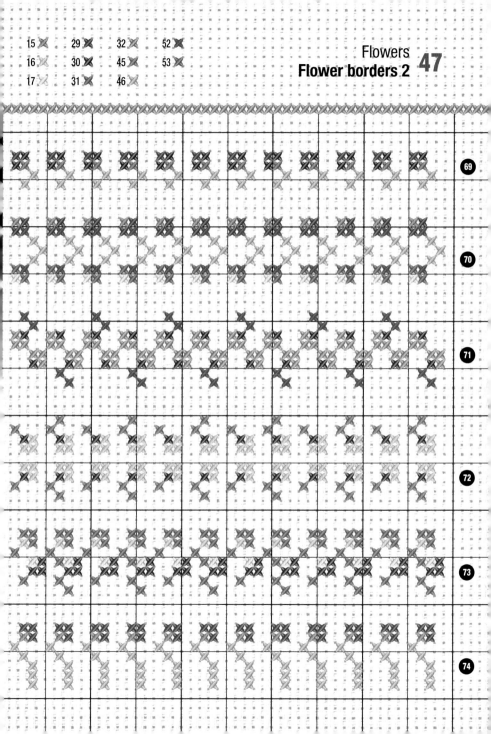

48 Flowers
Flower borders 3

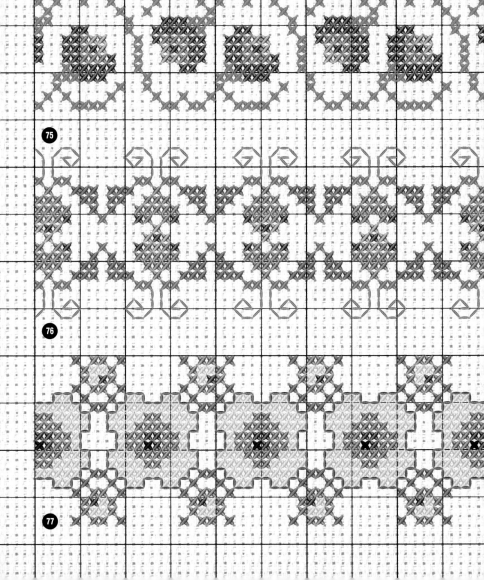

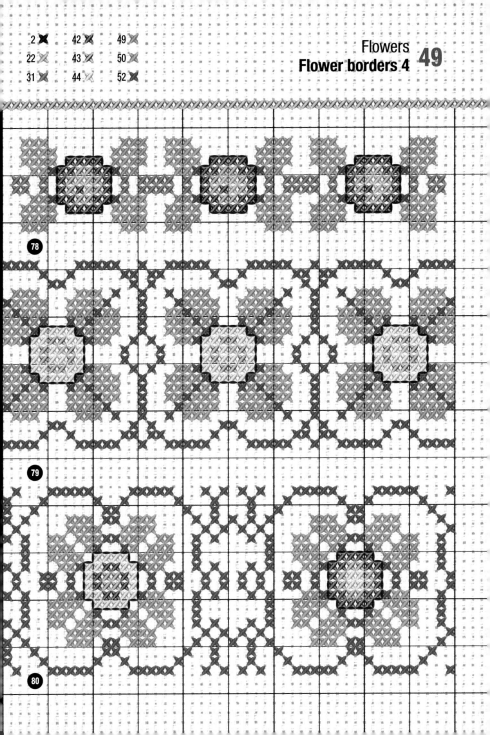

50 Home and garden
Country garden 1

✖ 2　✖ 20　✖ 27　✖ 33　✖ 51
✖ 13　✖ 23　✖ 28　✖ 45　✖ 52
✖ 19　✖ 24　✖ 31　✖ 46

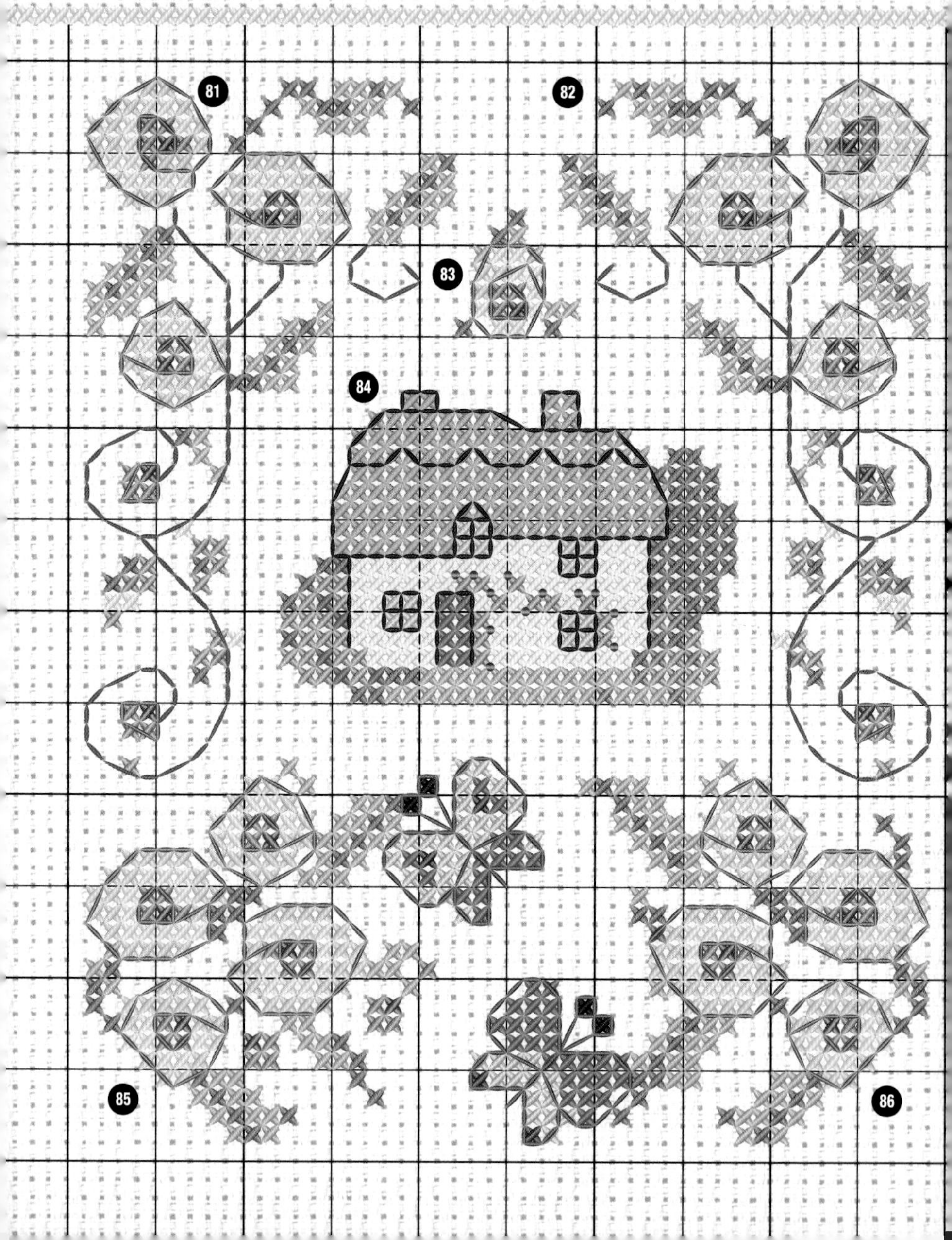

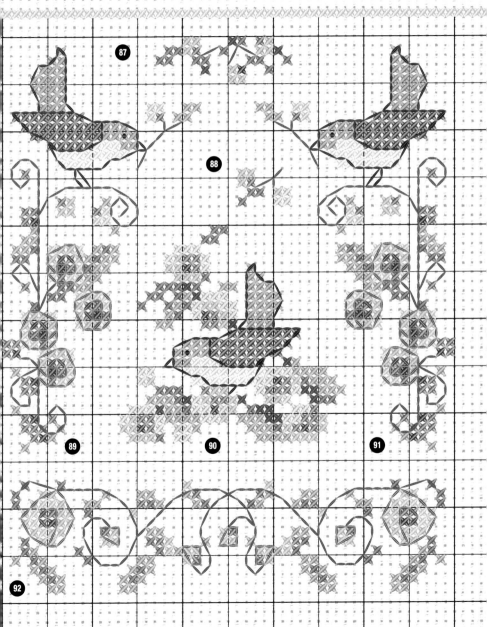

1	✕ 5	✕ 12	✕ 19	✕ 50
✕ 2	✕ 7	✕ 13	✕ 20	✕ 51
✕ 4	✕ 11	✕ 14	✕ 42	

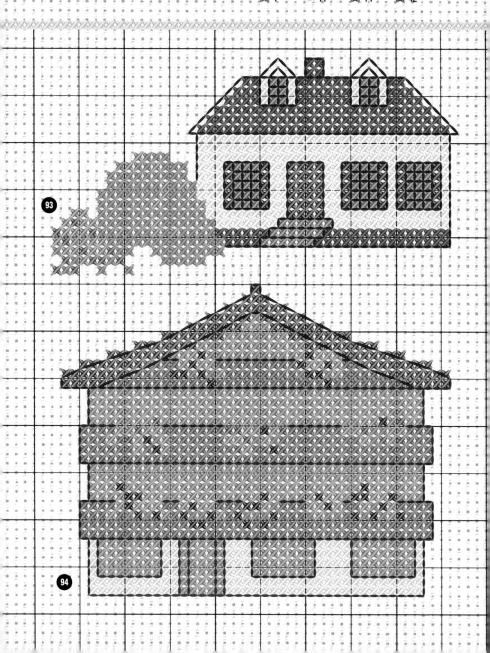

93

94

2 ✖   8 ✖   20 ✖   33 ✖   47 ✖
4 ✖   11 ✖   24 ✖   45 ✖   56 ✖
5 ✖   12 ✖   31 ✖   46 ✖

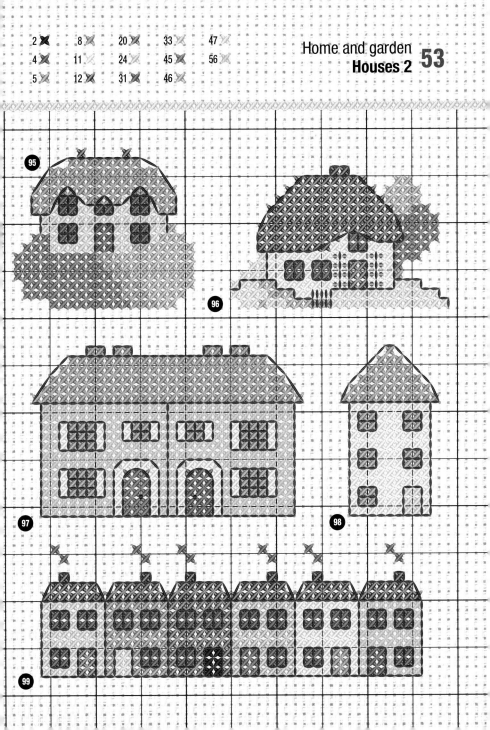

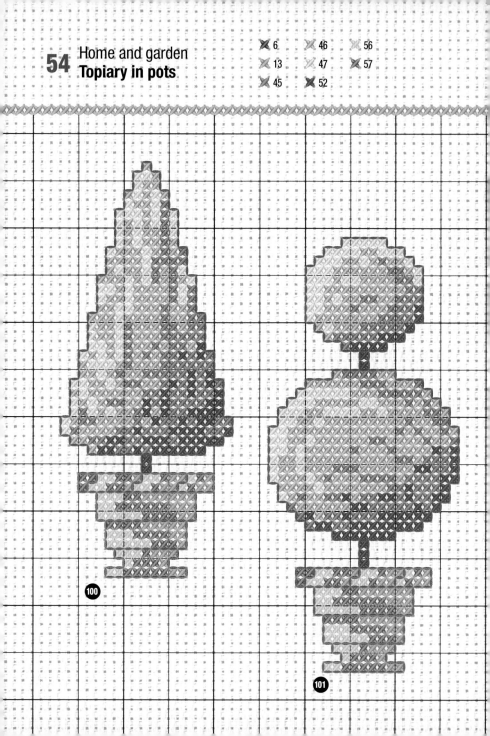

1   5   11   30
2   9   12
3   10   13

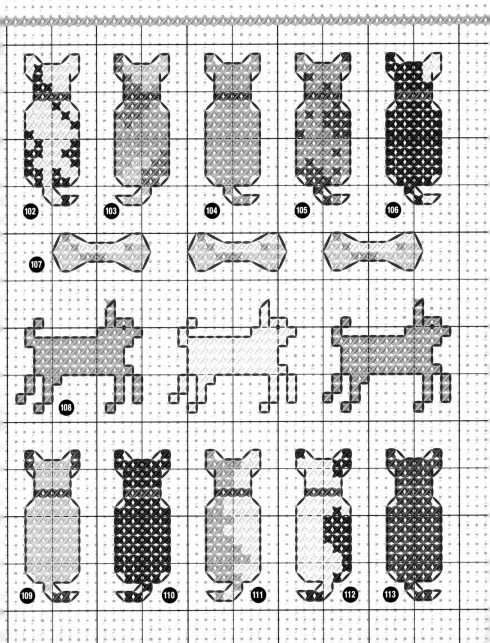

1	7	12	24	50
2	8	13	32	
4	11	14	34	

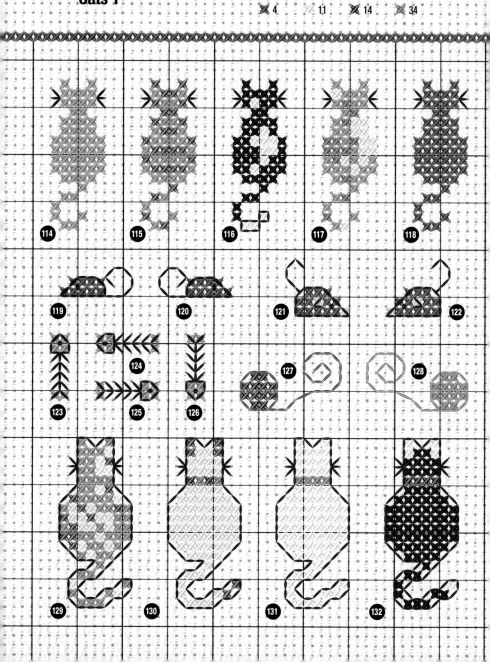

1   5   12   31
2   8   13   50
4   11   15

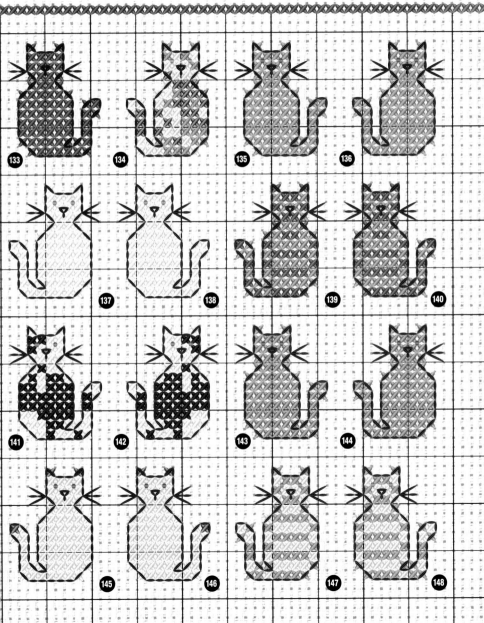

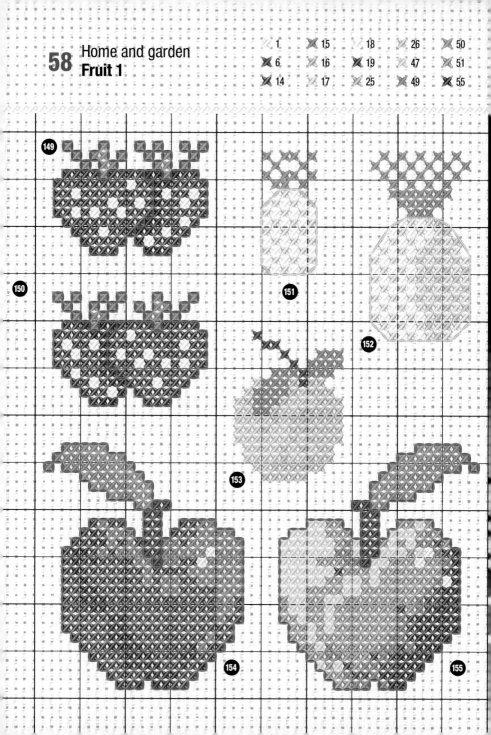

6 ✖   16 ✖   19 ✖   46 ✖   52 ✖
11 ✖   17 ✖   42 ✖   47 ✖   55 ✖
15 ✖   18   45 ✖   49 ✖

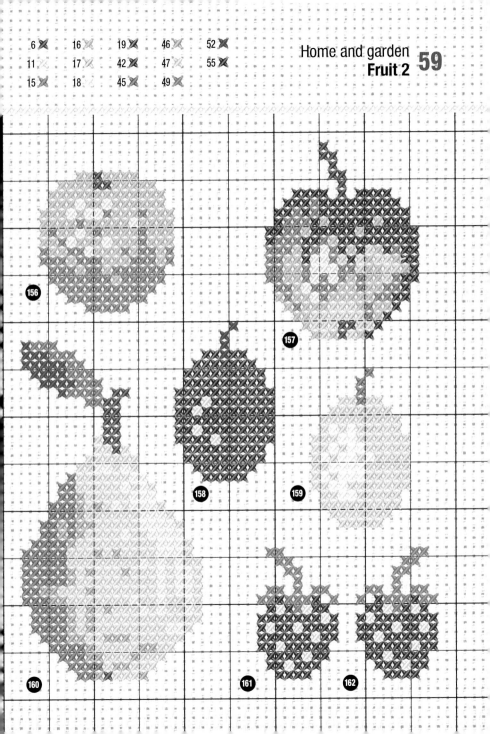

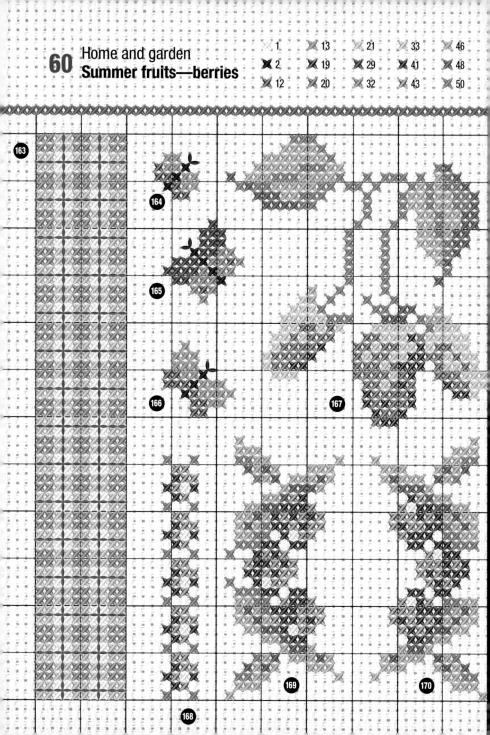

60 Home and garden
Summer fruits—berries

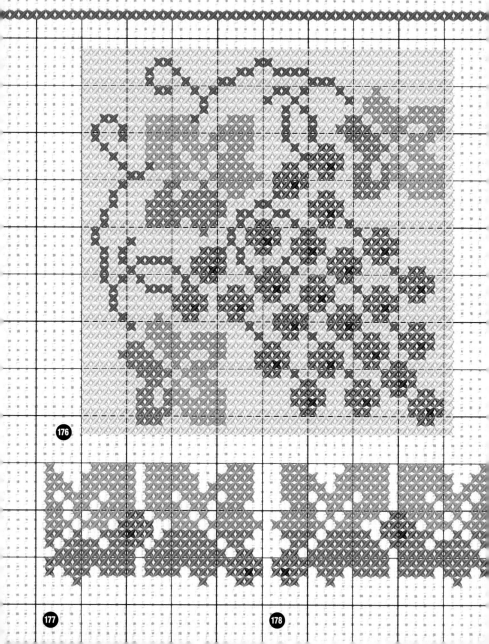

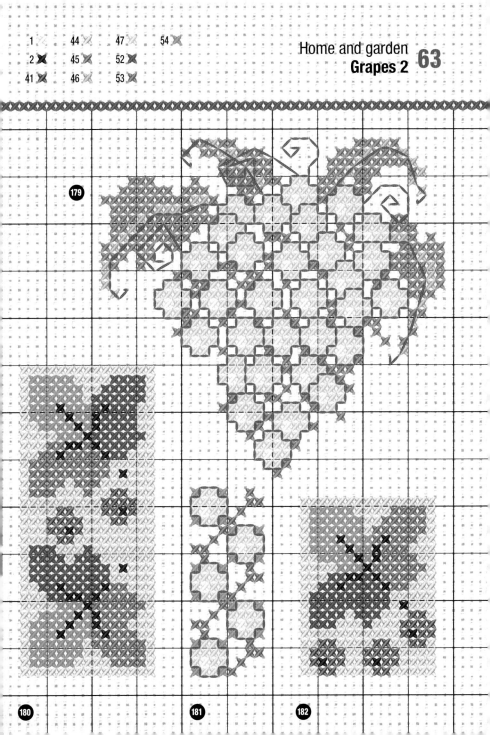

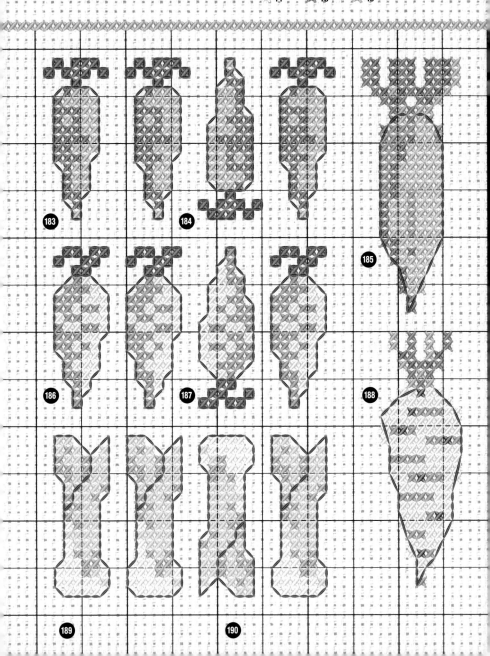

1	14	47	51
5	45	49	52
10	46	50	55

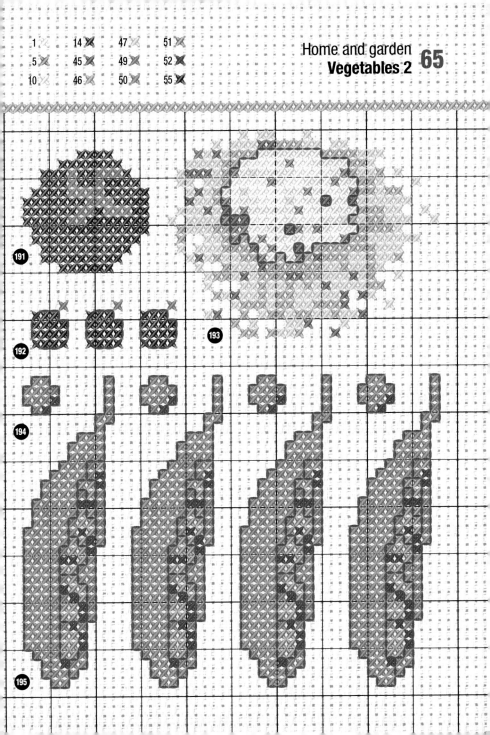

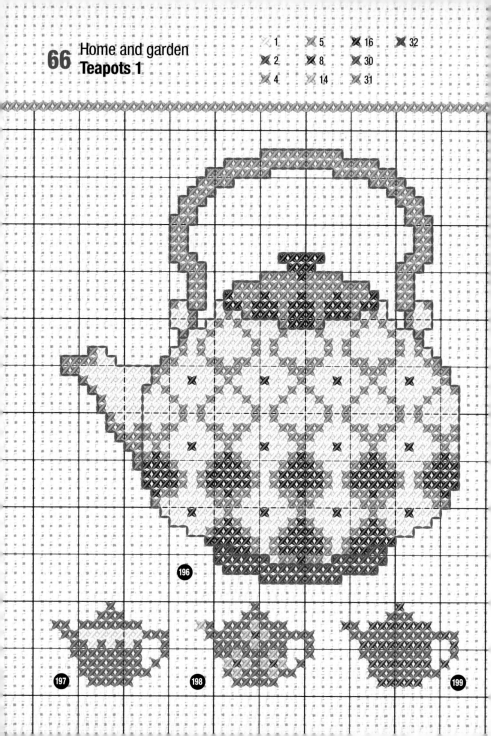

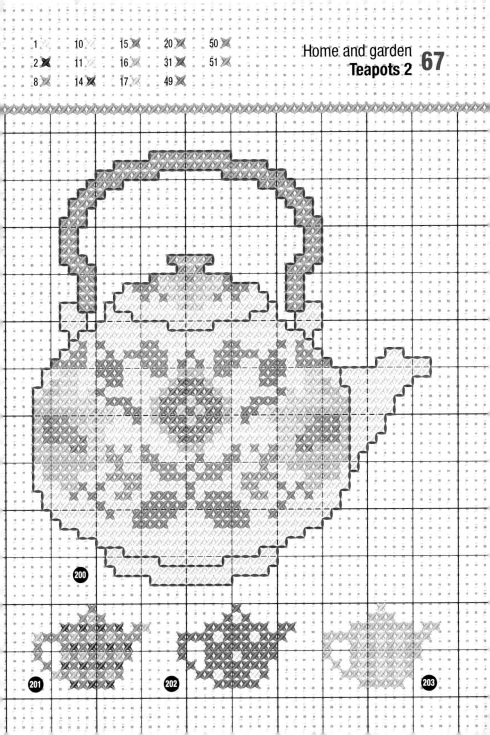

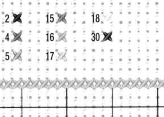

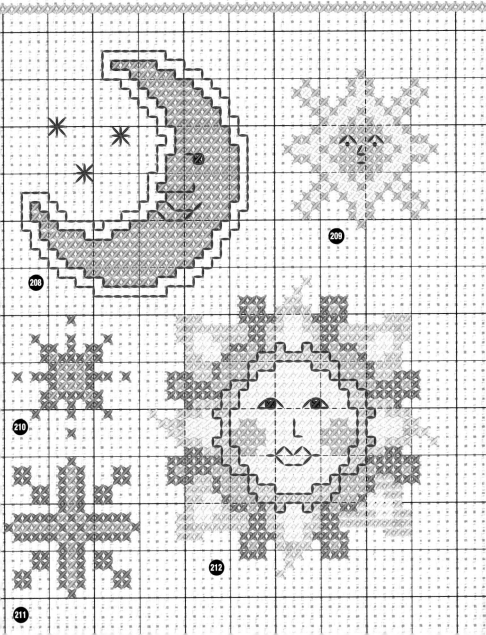

✕	1	✕	7	✕	15	✕	51
✕	2	✕	8	✕	16	✕	55
✕	6	✕	11	✕	50		

213
214
215
216
217
218

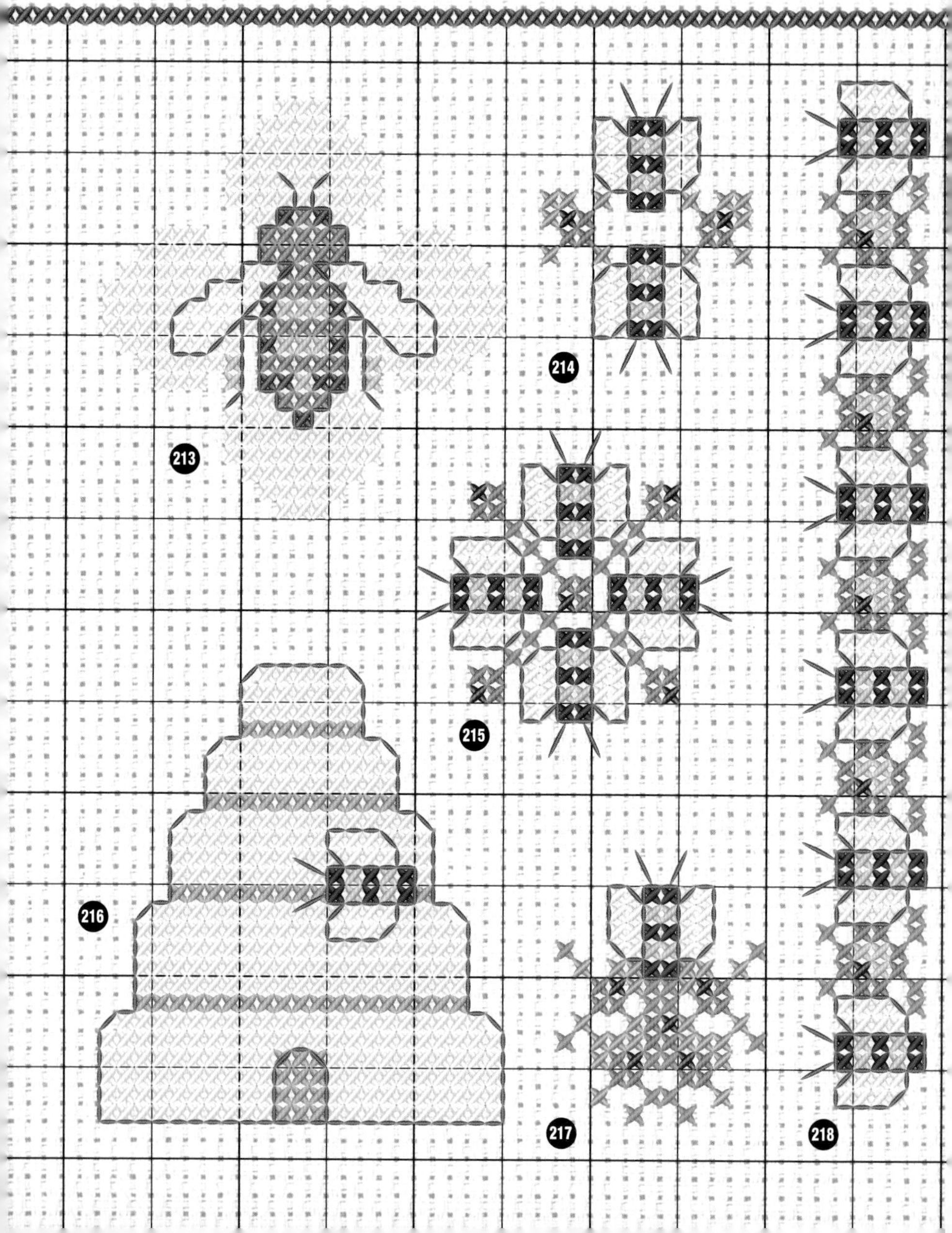

1   9   13   36

2   11   14   40

6   12   35

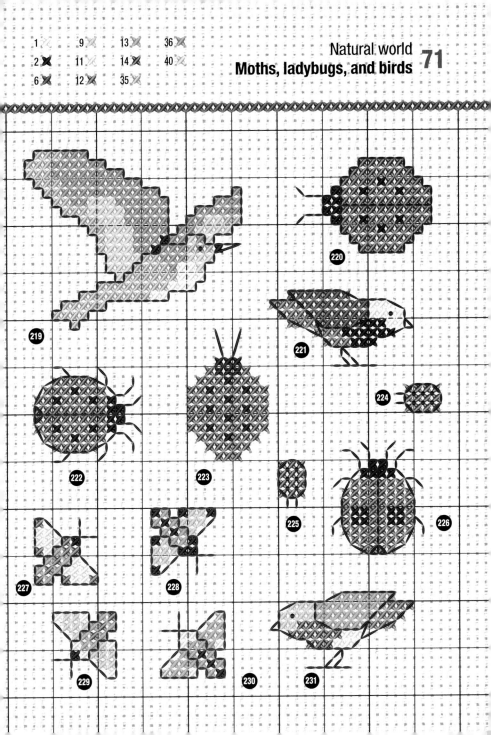

✗ 3

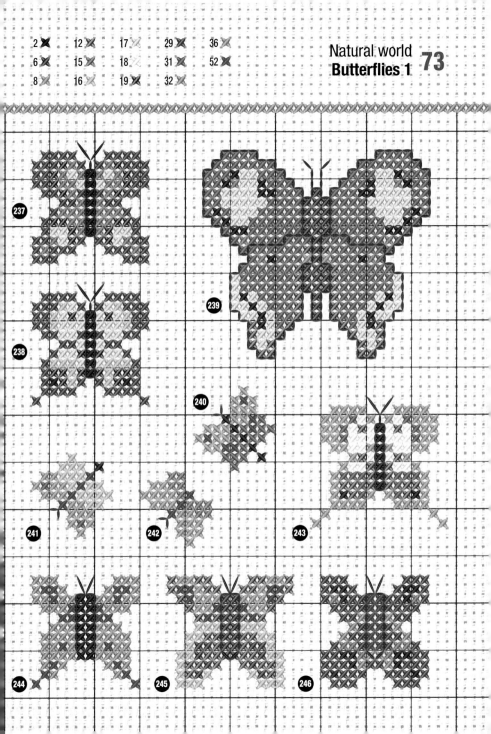

✖ 2	✖ 12	✖ 15	✖ 31	
✖ 6	✖ 13	✖ 17	✖ 32	
✖ 7	✖ 14	✖ 18	✖ 52	

2 ✖ 12 ✖ 17 ✖ 29 ✖ 55 ✖
6 ✖ 13 ✖ 18 ✖ 31 ✖
8 ✖ 16 ✖ 28 ✖ 32 ✖

2 ✖ 10 ✖ 22 ✖ 33 ✖ 47 ✖
6 ✖ 17 ✖ 27 ✖ 38 ✖
7 ✖ 18 ✖ 32 ✖ 40 ✖

258

259

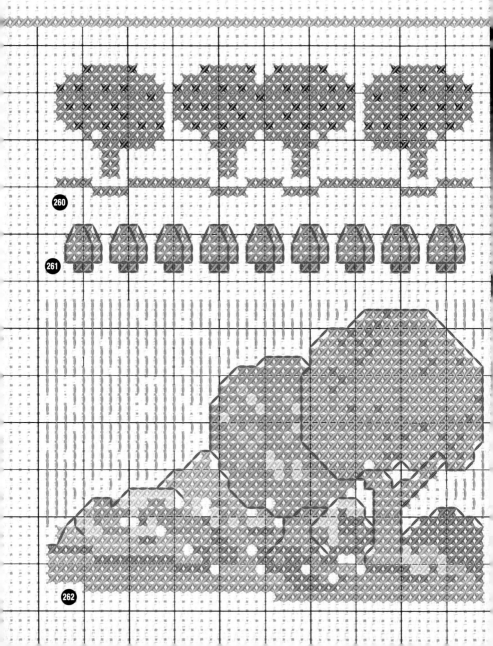

6	13	45
7	16	46
12	17	52

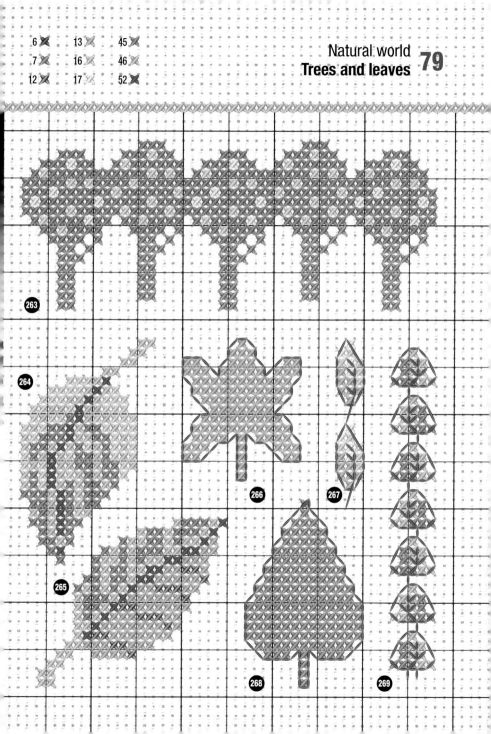

263

264

266

267

265

268

269

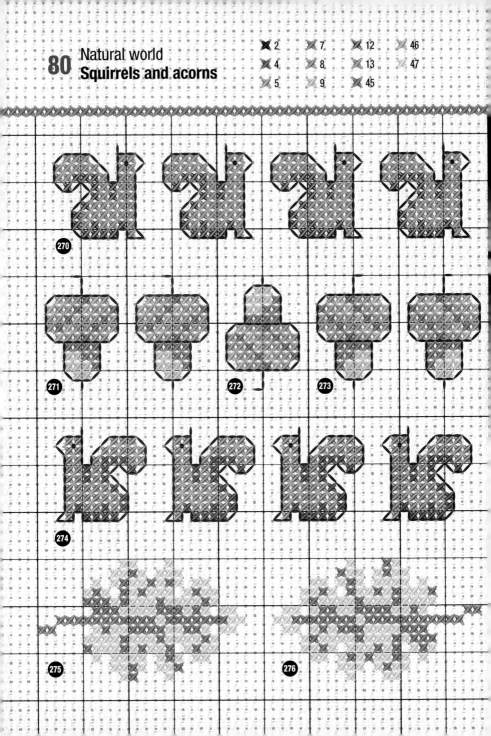

80 Natural world
Squirrels and acorns

✖ 2		✖ 7		✖ 12		✖ 46	
✖ 4		✖ 8		✖ 13		✖ 47	
✖ 5		✖ 9		✖ 45			

270

271 272 273

274

275 276

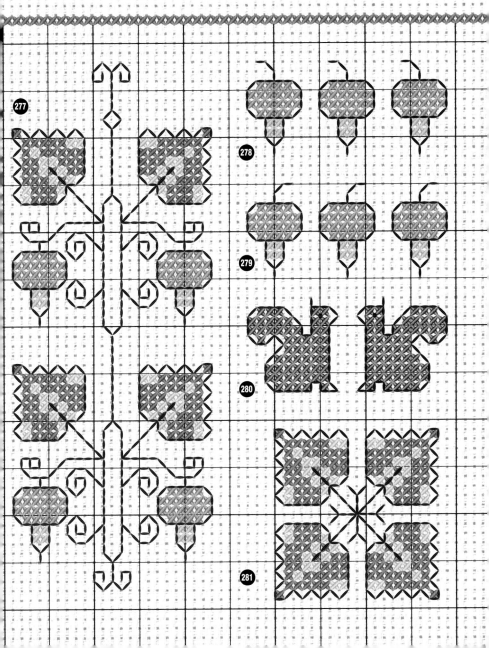

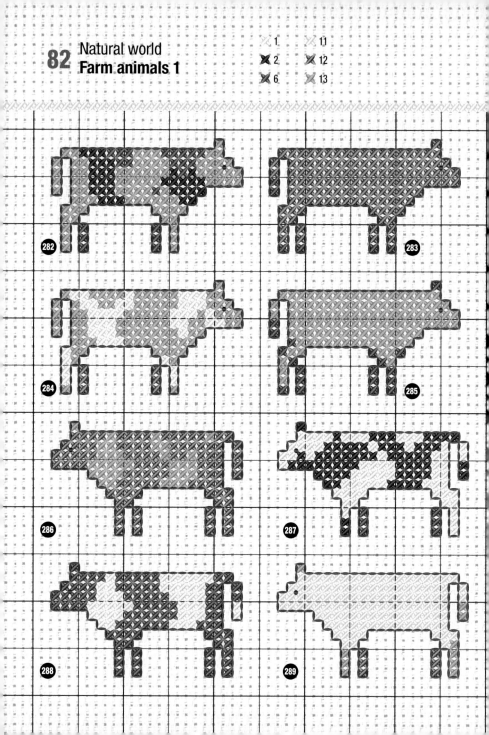

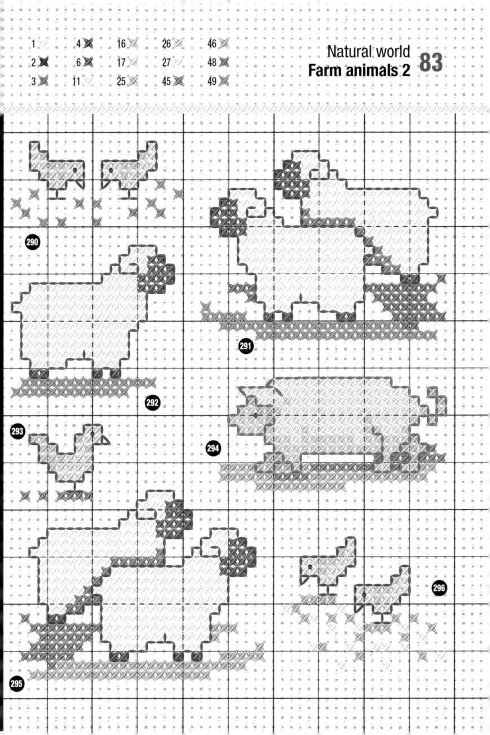

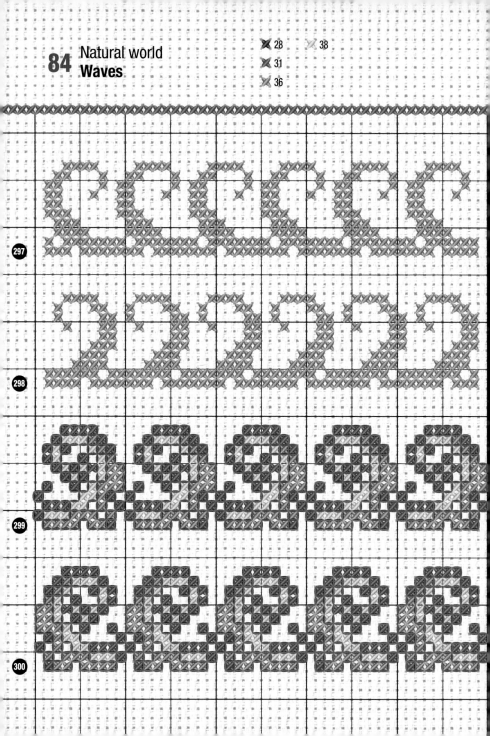

84 Natural world
Waves

297

298

299

300

2 ✖ 30 ✖ 35 ✖ 50 ✖
16 ✖ 31 ✖ 39 ✖ 51 ✖
17 ✖ 32 ✖ 40 ✖

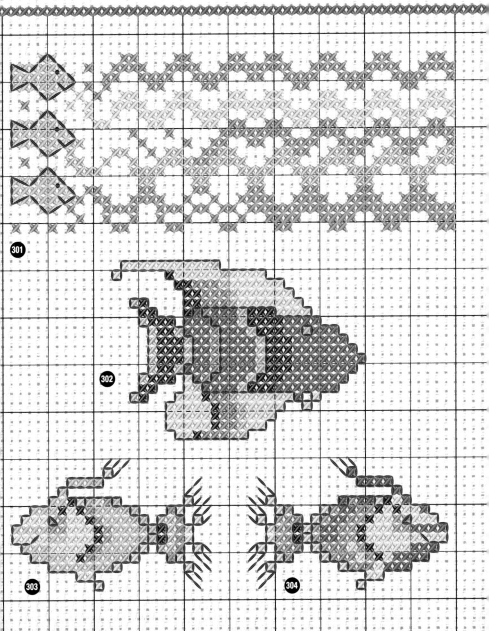

301

302

303

304

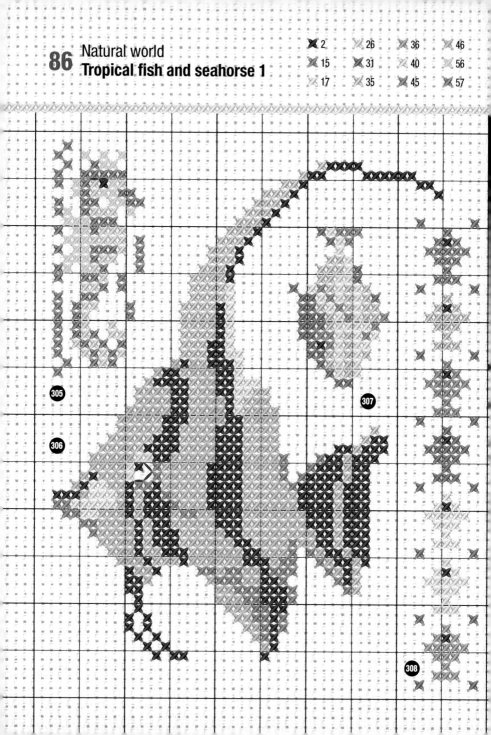

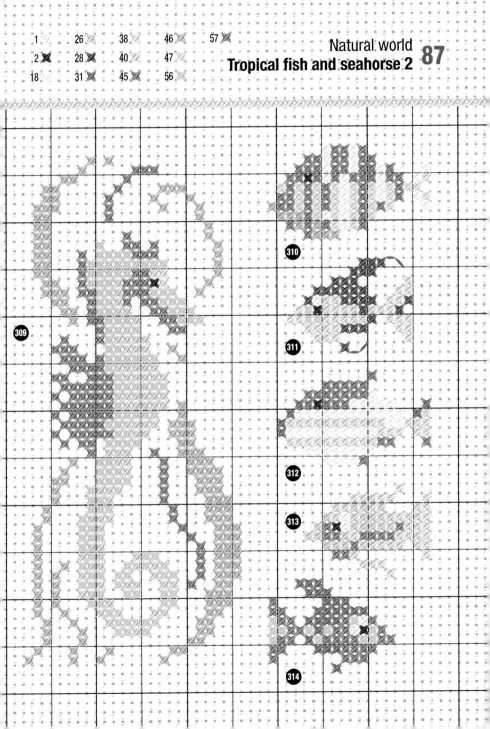

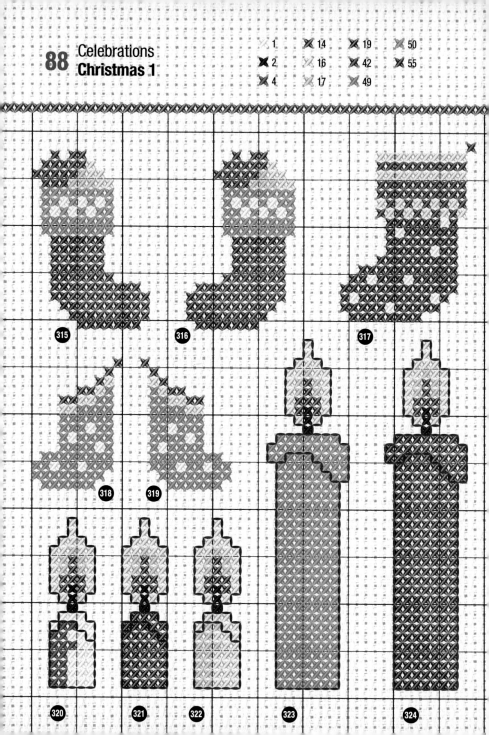

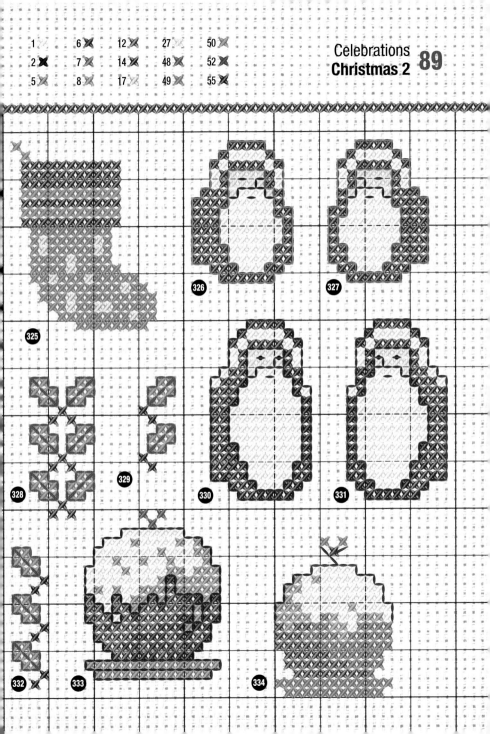

1   5 ✕   17 ✕   49 ✕   55 ✕
2 ✕   14 ✕   18   50 ✕
4 ✕   15 ✕   19 ✕   51 ✕

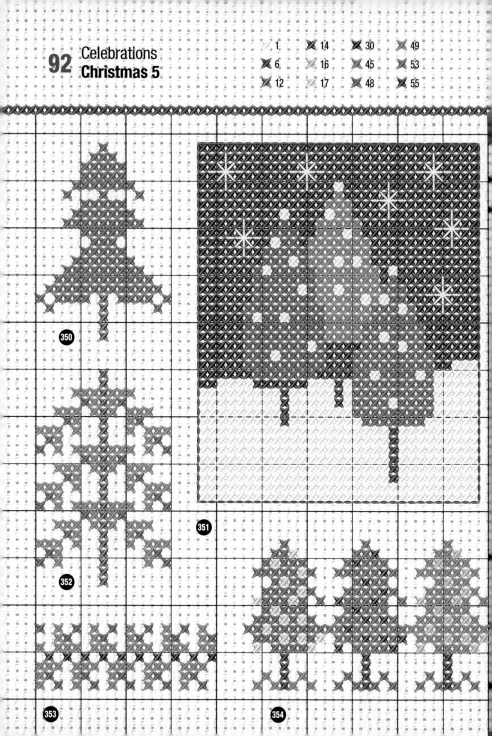

6 ✕   16 ✕   34 ✕   50 ✕   54 ✕
12 ✕   17 ✕   48 ✕   51 ✕   55 ✕
14 ✕   18 ✕   49 ✕   53 ✕

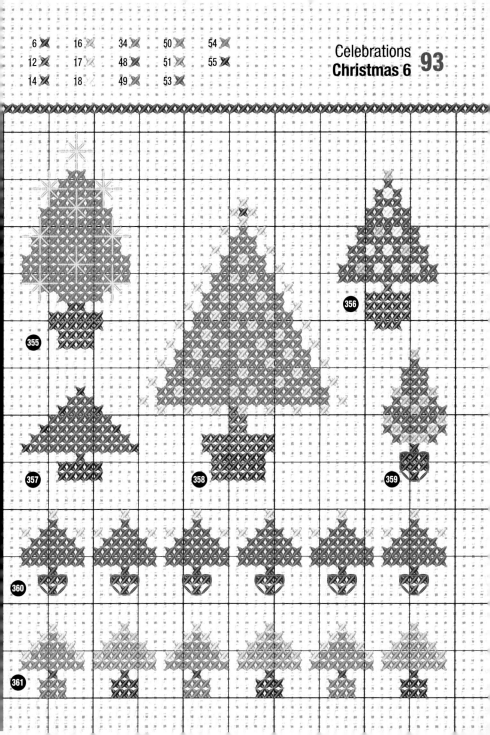

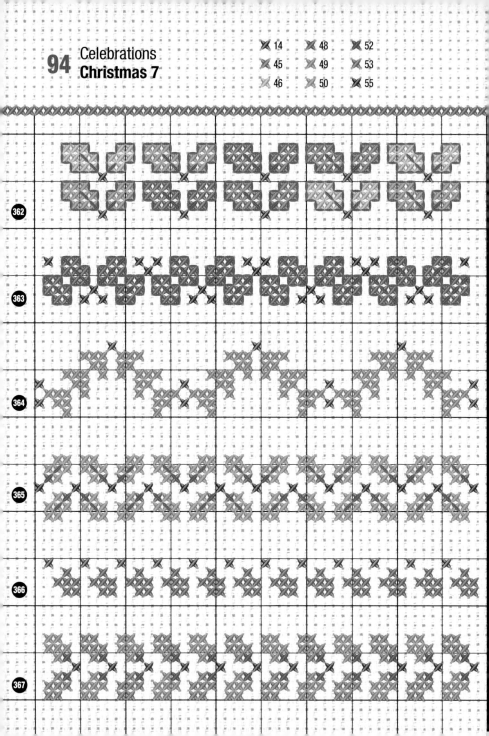

✖ 14 ✖ 48 ✖ 52
✖ 45 ✖ 49 ✖ 53
✖ 46 ✖ 50 ✖ 55

362

363

364

365

366

367

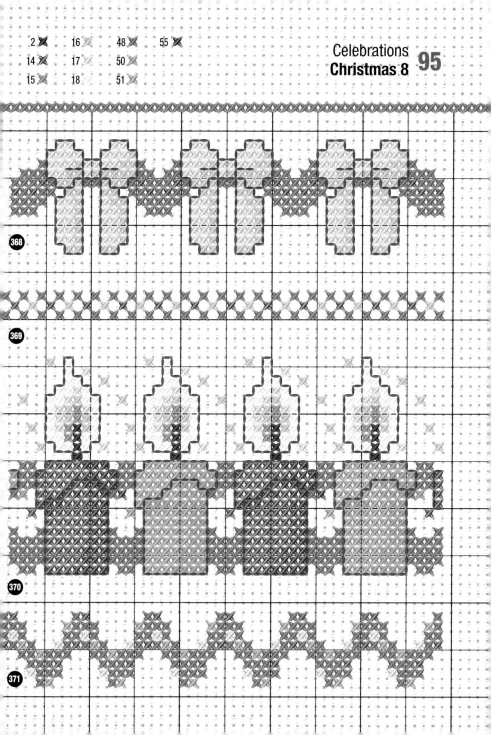

✕ 3	✕ 15	✕ 21	✕ 25	✕ 44
✕ 11	✕ 19	✕ 22	✕ 42	✕ 45
✕ 14	✕ 20	✕ 24	✕ 43	✕ 50

372
373
374
375
376
377
378
379
380
381
382
383

	1		19 ✖		23 ✖		42 ✖
	10		20 ✖		24 ✖		43 ✖
	14 ✖		21 ✖		25 ✖		44 ✖

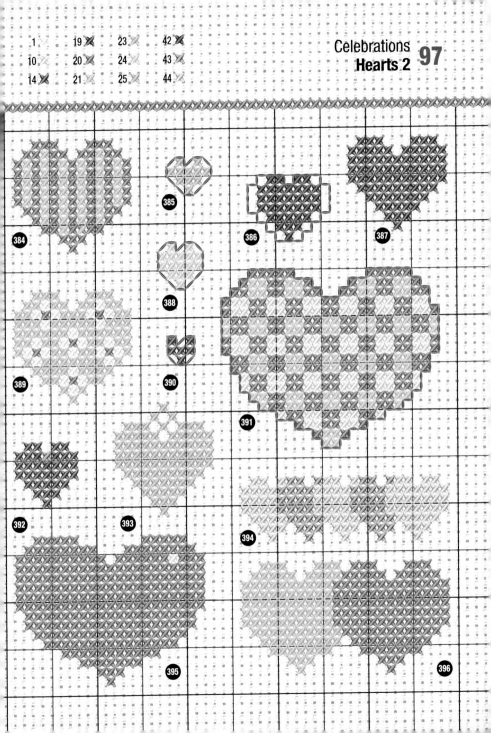

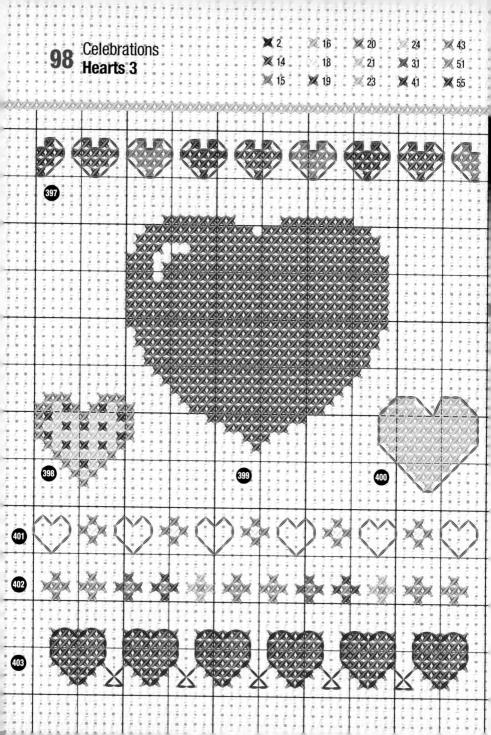

✗ 2   ✗ 16   ✗ 20   ✗ 24   ✗ 43
✗ 14   ✗ 18   ✗ 21   ✗ 31   ✗ 51
✗ 15   ✗ 19   ✗ 23   ✗ 41   ✗ 55

397

398   399   400

401

402

403

2 ✗ 14 ✗ 21 ✗ 41 ✗ 53 ✗
4 ✗ 19 ✗ 22 ✗ 43 ✗ 55 ✗
11 ✗ 20 ✗ 24 ✗ 44 ✗

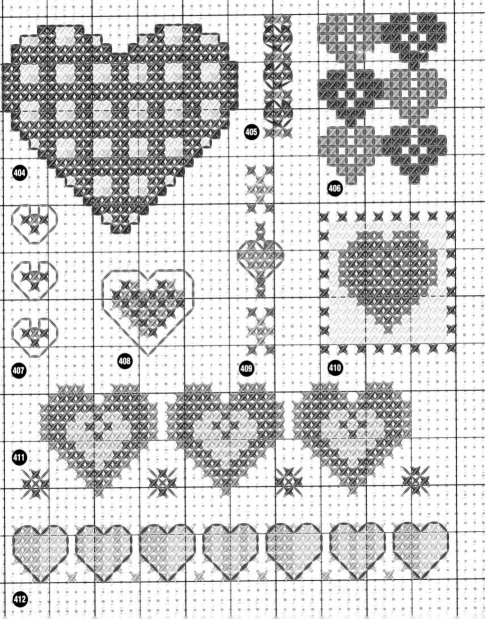

Easter 1

1	16	45	50
11	17	46	52
15	18	49	

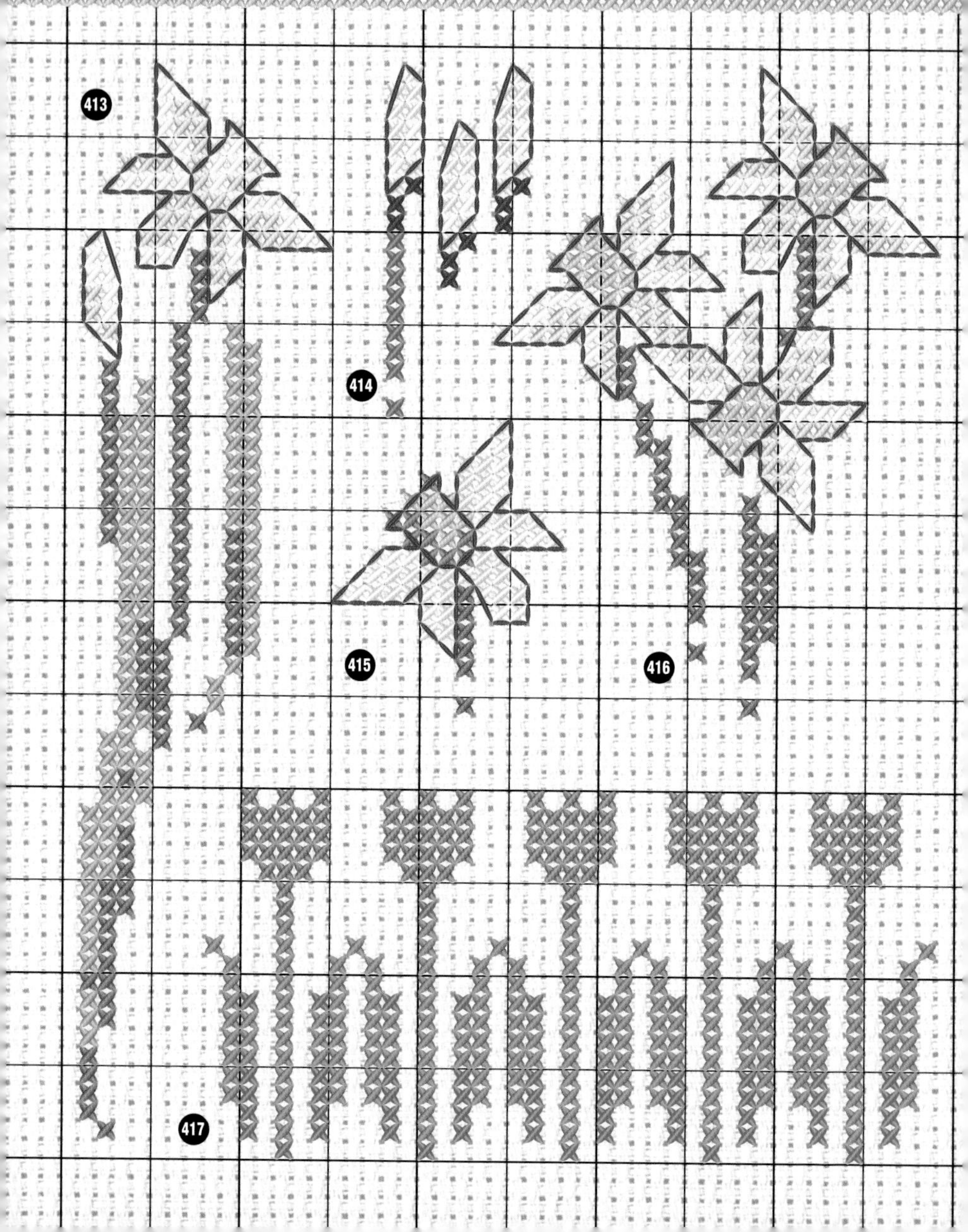

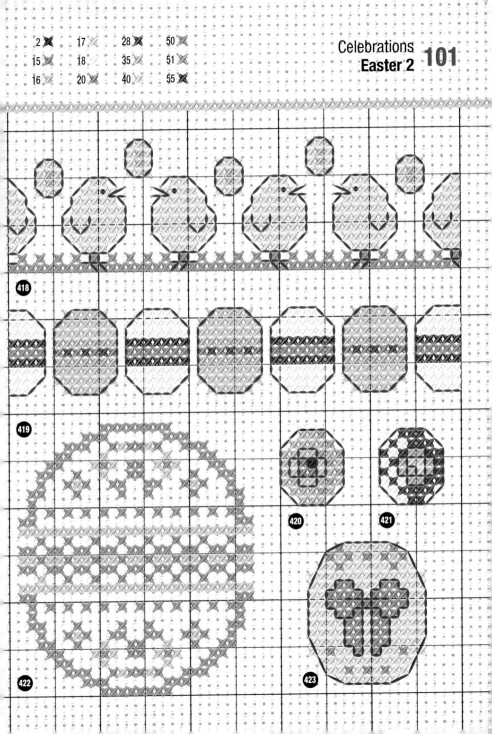

2 ✕ 17 ✕ 28 ✕ 50 ✕
15 ✕ 18 35 ✕ 51 ✕
16 ✕ 20 ✕ 40 ✕ 55 ✕

418

419

420 421

422 423

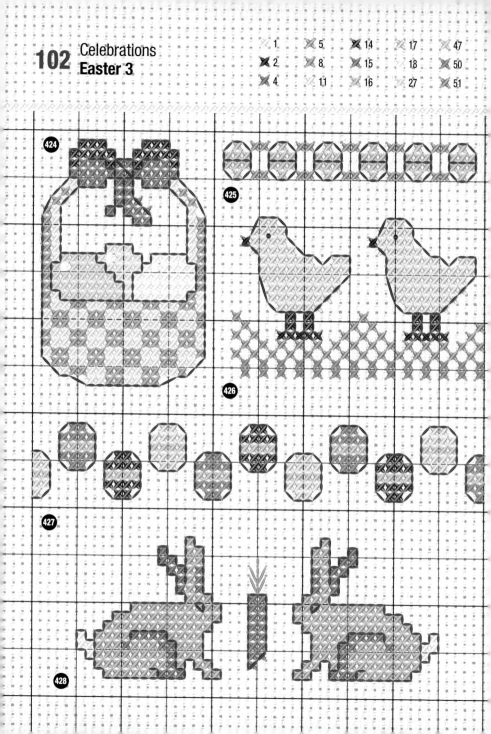

2 ✖   17 ✖   40 ✖   52 ✖
14 ✖   18 ✖   50 ✖   55 ✖
16 ✖   32 ✖   51 ✖

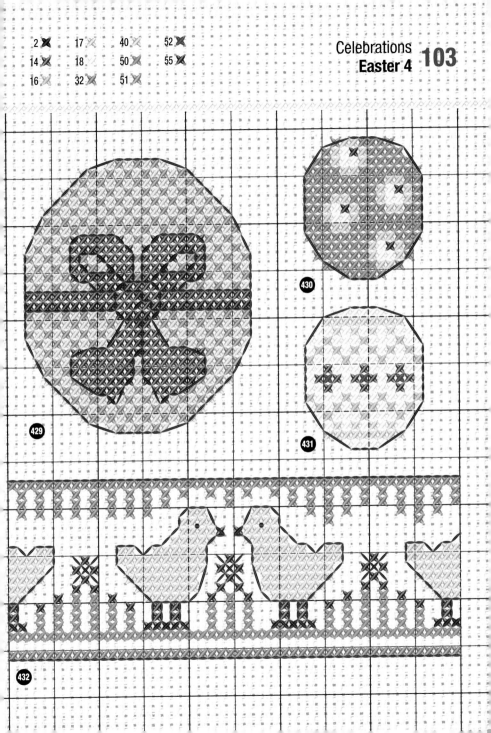

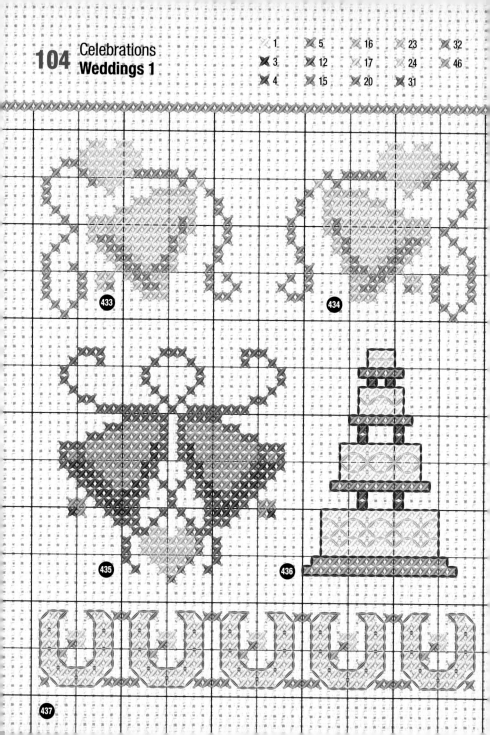

⊠ 1	⊠ 5	⊠ 16	⊠ 23	⊠ 32
⊠ 3	⊠ 12	⊠ 17	⊠ 24	⊠ 46
⊠ 4	⊠ 15	⊠ 20	⊠ 31	

433

434

435

436

437

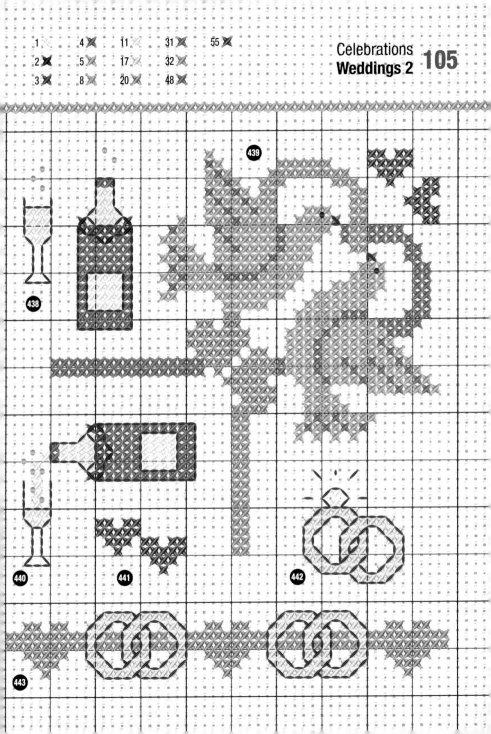

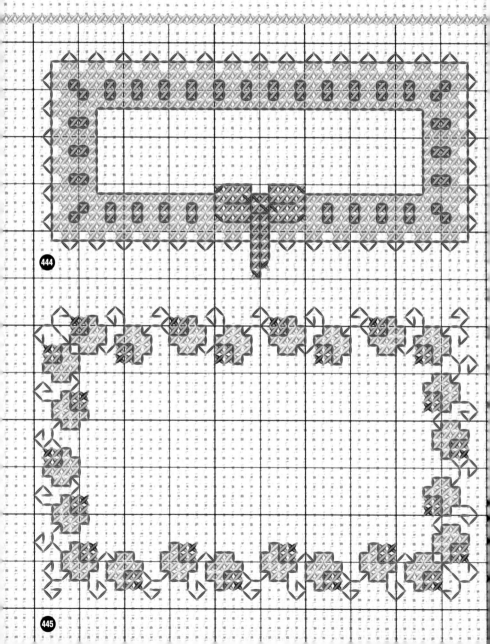

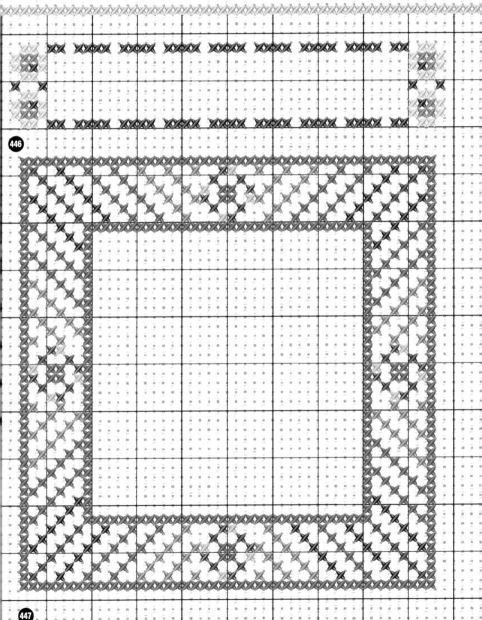

108 Cultures
Indian borders 1

8 11 16 17 20 35 39 42 51 55

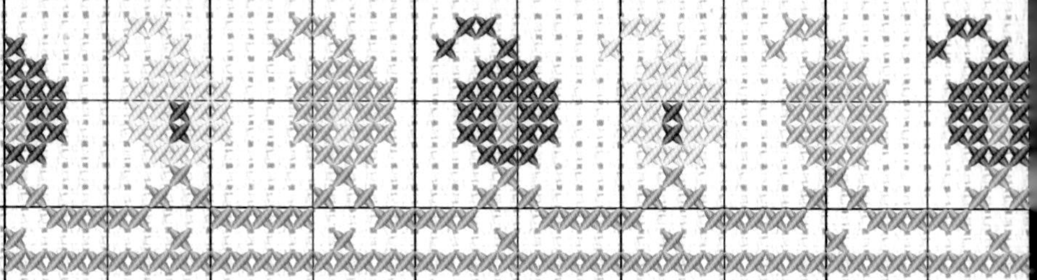

448

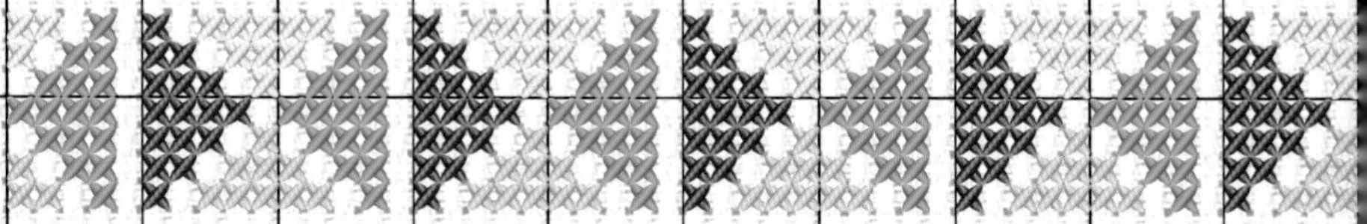

449

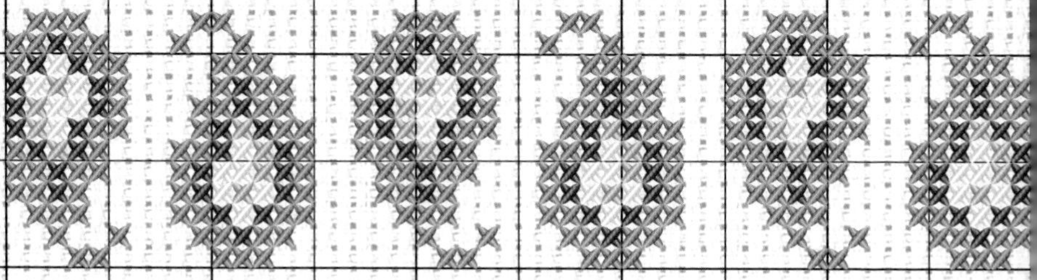

450

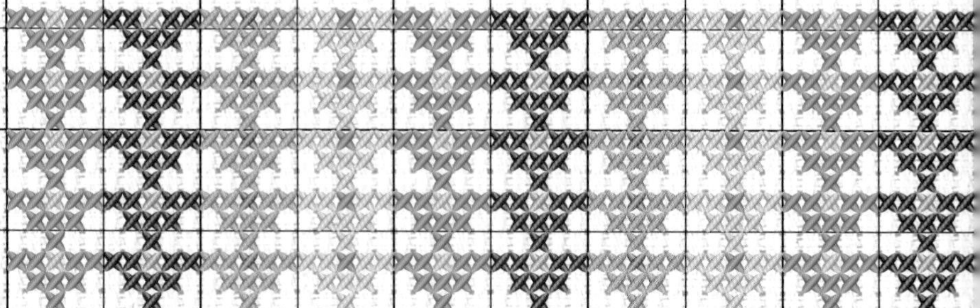

451

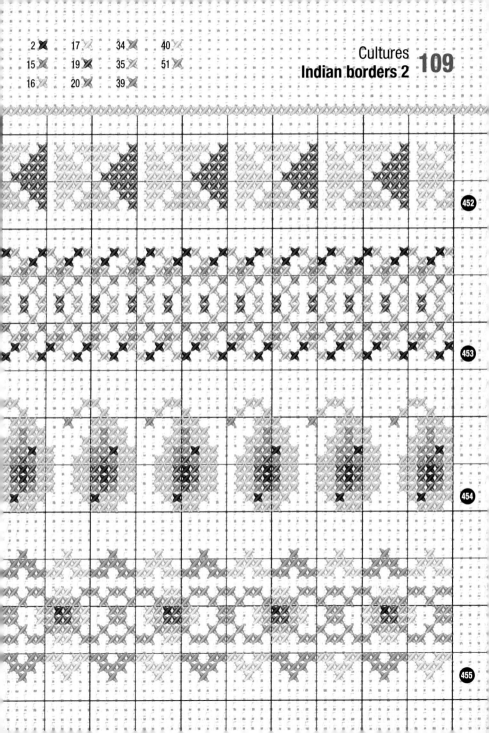

2 ✕   17 ✕   34 ✕   40 ✕
15 ✕   19 ✕   35 ✕   51 ✕
16 ✕   20 ✕   39 ✕

452
453
454
455

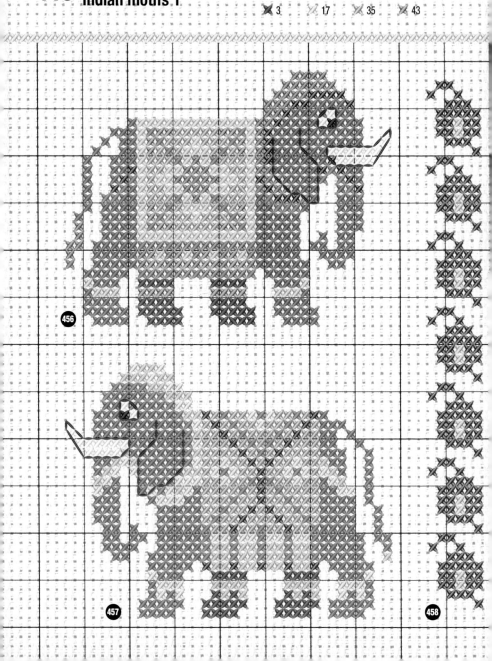

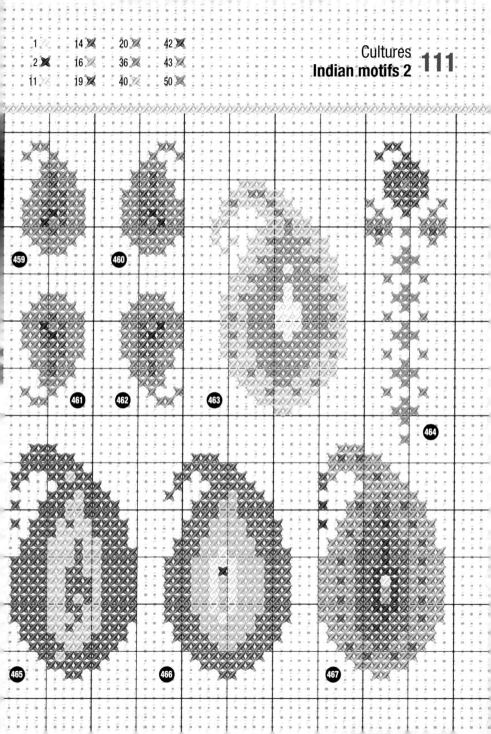

1   14 ✖   20 ✖   42 ✖
2 ✖   16 ✖   36 ✖   43 ✖
11   19 ✖   40 ✖   50 ✖

459 460 461 462 463 464 465 466 467

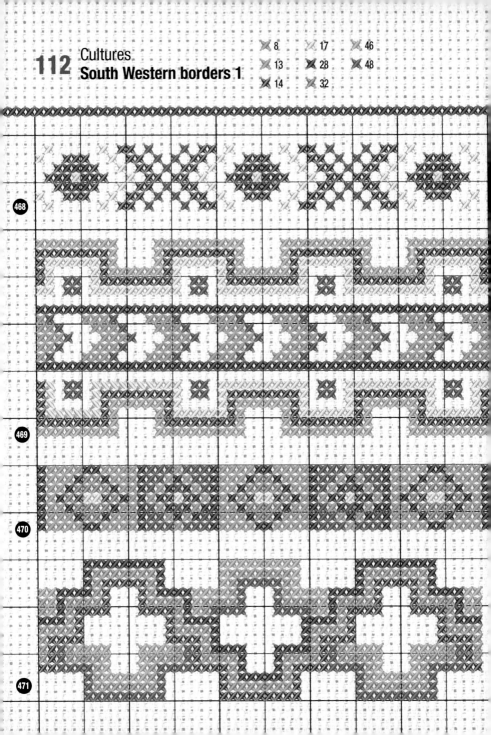

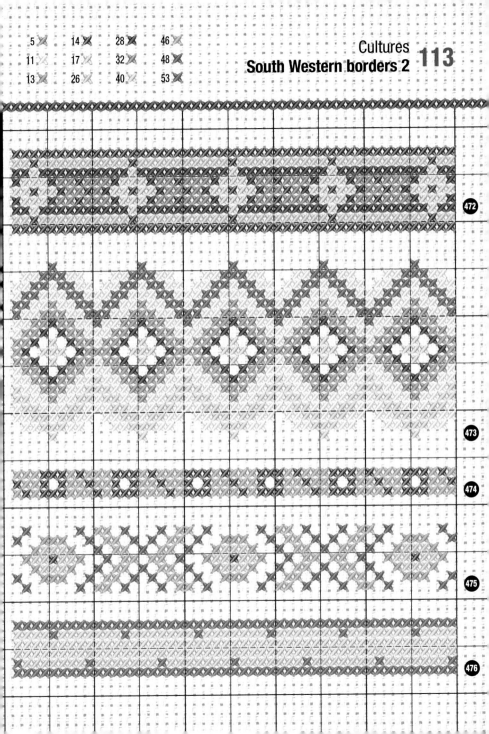

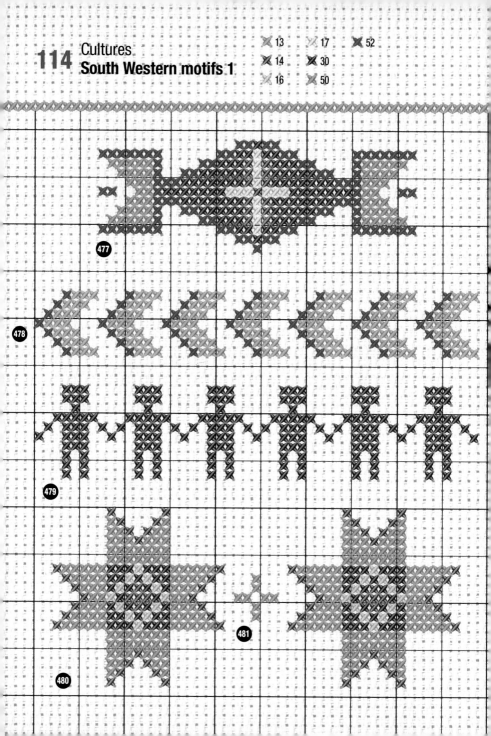

2 ✖ 16 ✖ 35 ✖
12 ✖ 17 ✖ 50 ✖
14 ✖ 30 ✖ 52 ✖

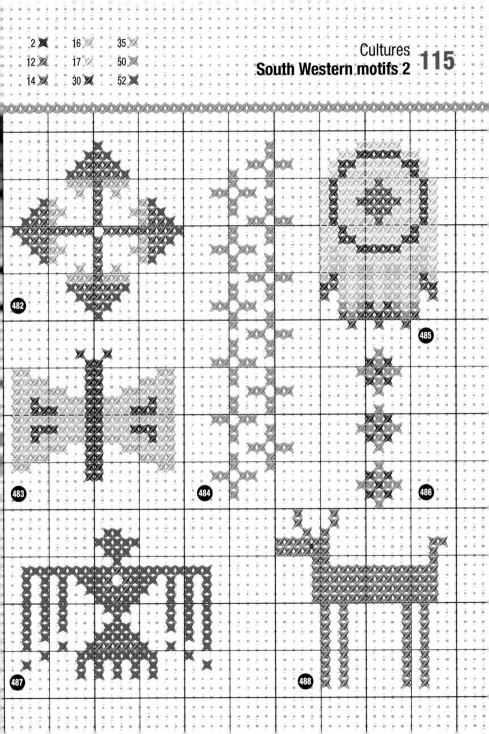

482

485

483

484

486

487

488

116 Cultures
Chinese designs 1

❌ 2 ❌ 31 ❌ 55
❌ 28 ❌ 32
❌ 29 ❌ 41

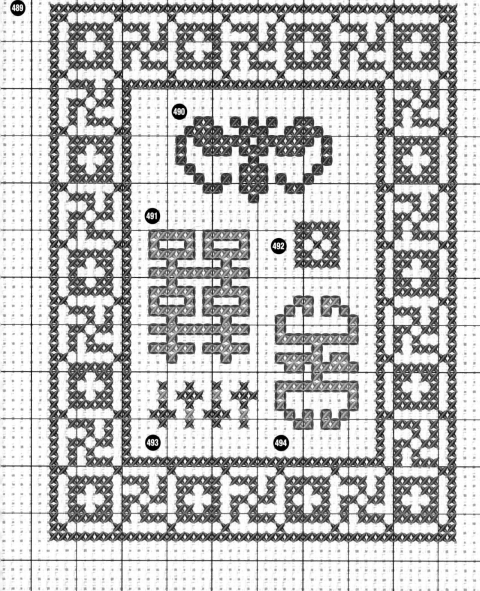

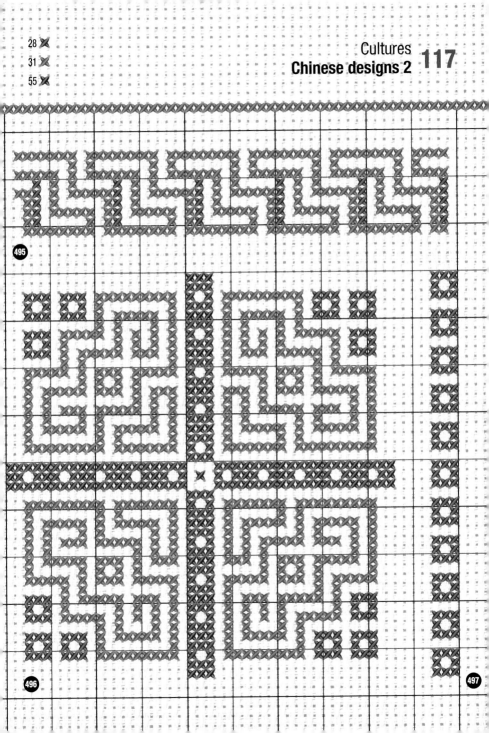

118 Cultures
Chinese designs 3

✖ 2   ✖ 31
✖ 28 ✖ 32
✖ 30 ✖ 55

498

499

500

501

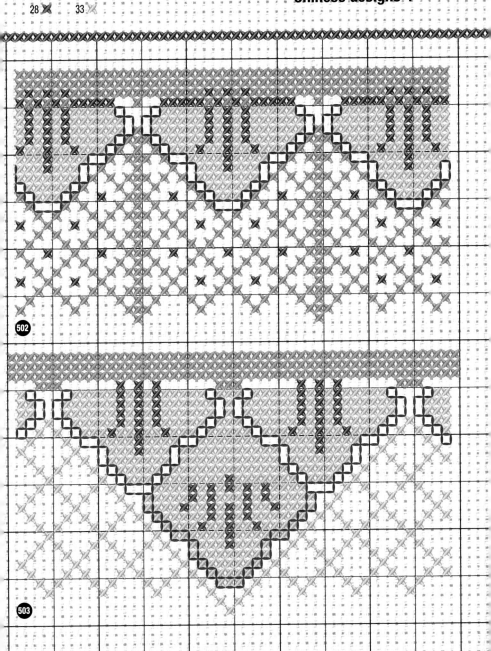

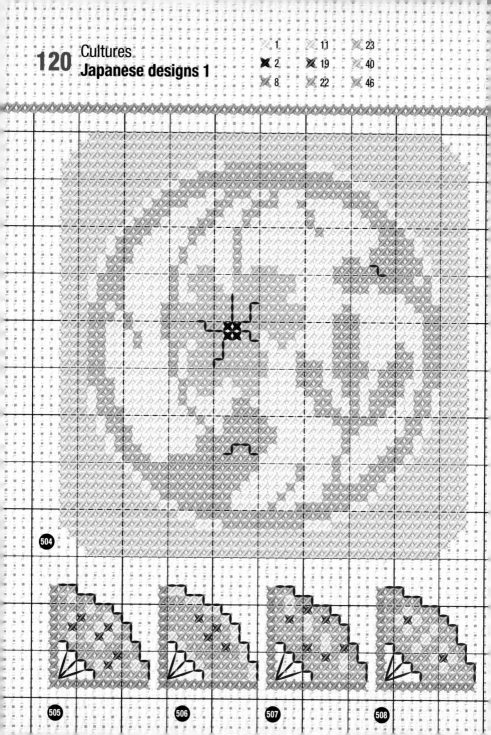

1
2
8
30
33

509

510   511   512   513

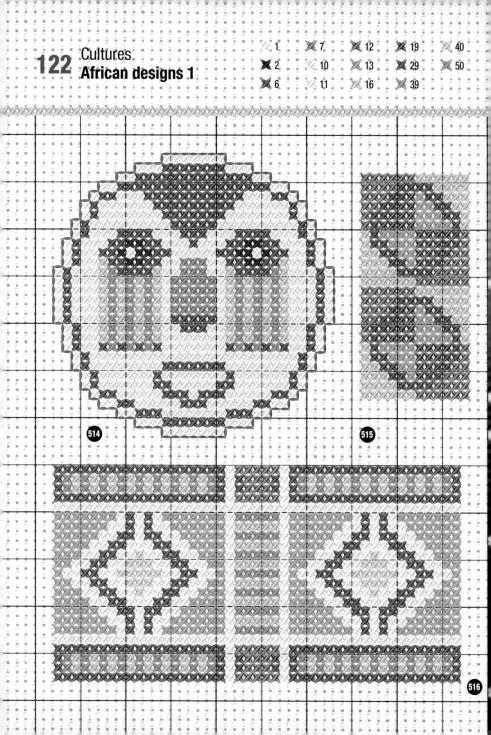

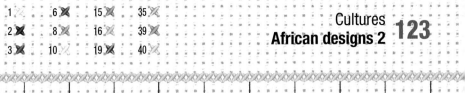

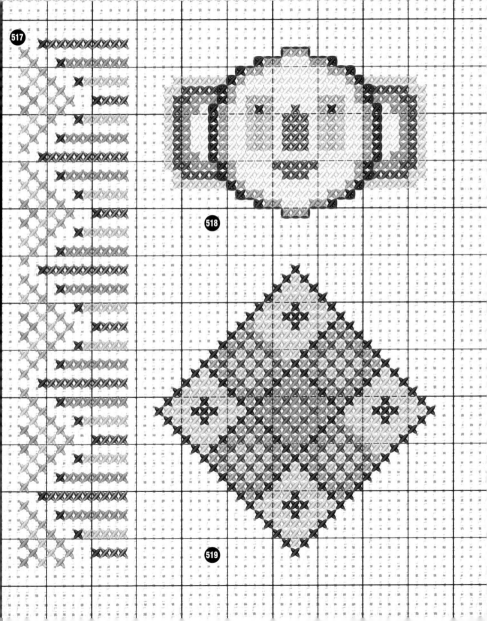

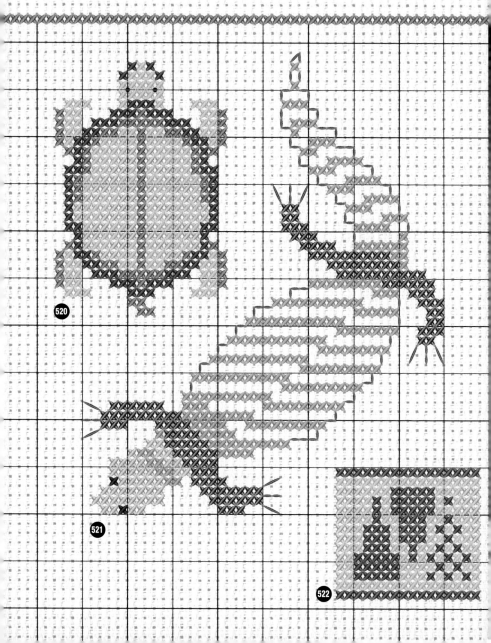

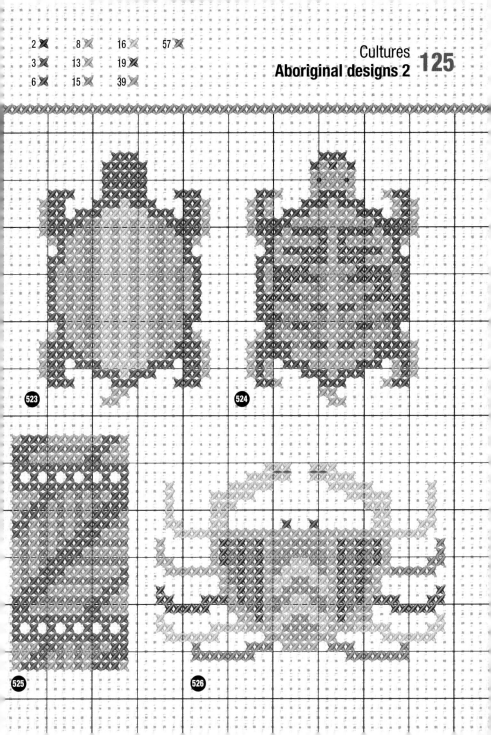

126 Cultures

South American borders 1

14 · 17 · 49

15 · 34

16 · 40

527
528
529
530

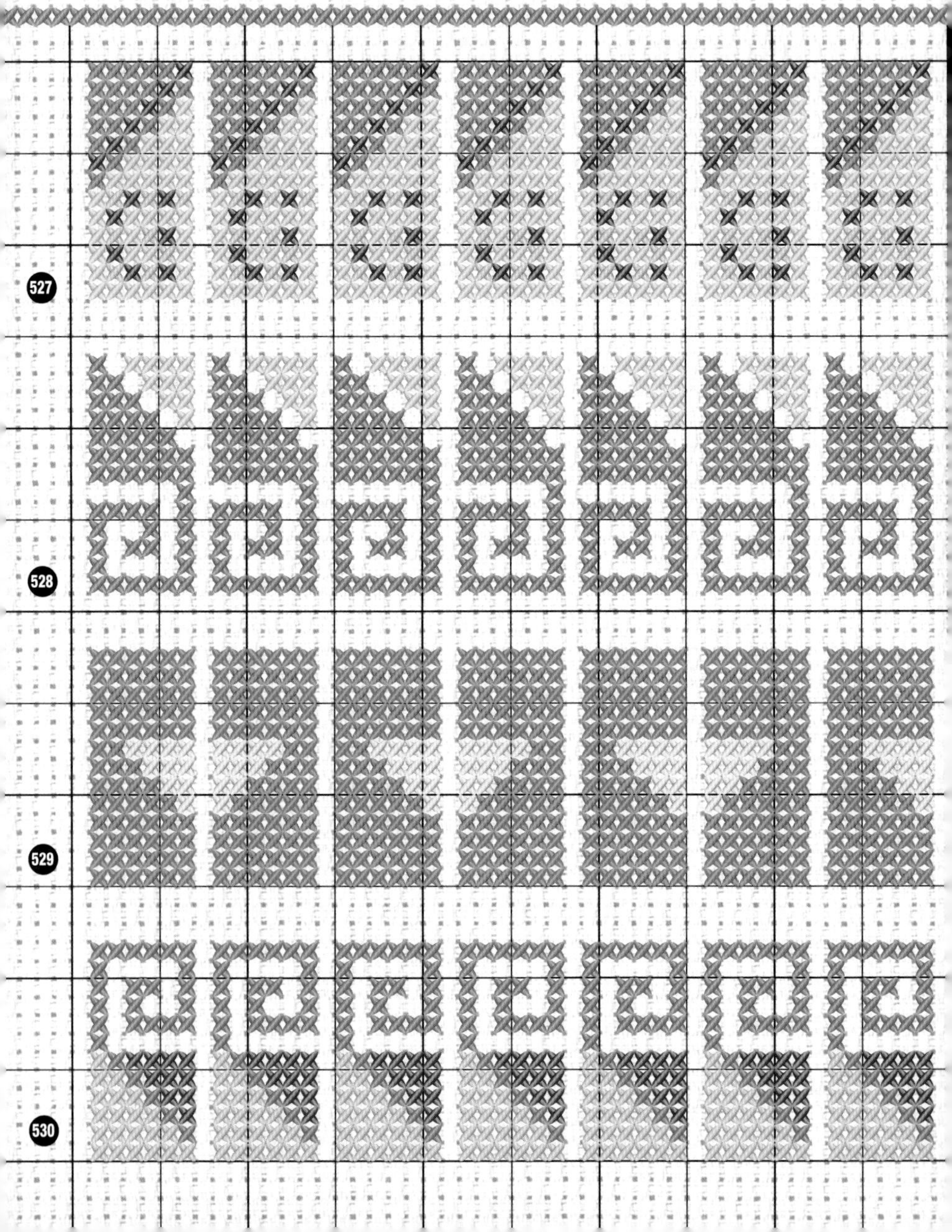

2 ✖ 16 ✖ 34 ✖
14 ✖ 17 ✖ 39 ✖
15 ✖ 18 ✖ 40 ✖

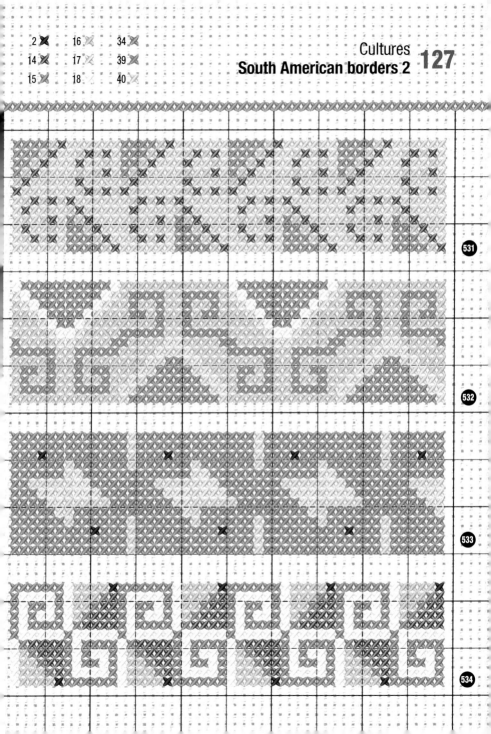

531

532

533

534

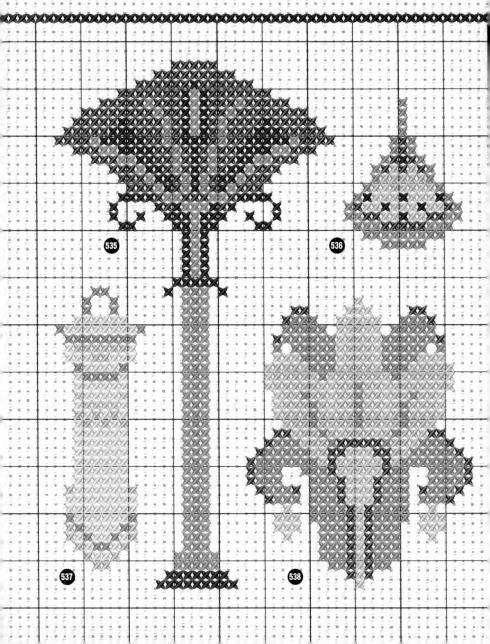

2 ✖	34 ✖	55 ✖
16 ✖	36 ✖	
17 ✖	50 ✖	

539

540

541

542

543

544

	1		16		35
✖	2		18		39
✖	4		34	✖	55

545

546

547   548   549

550

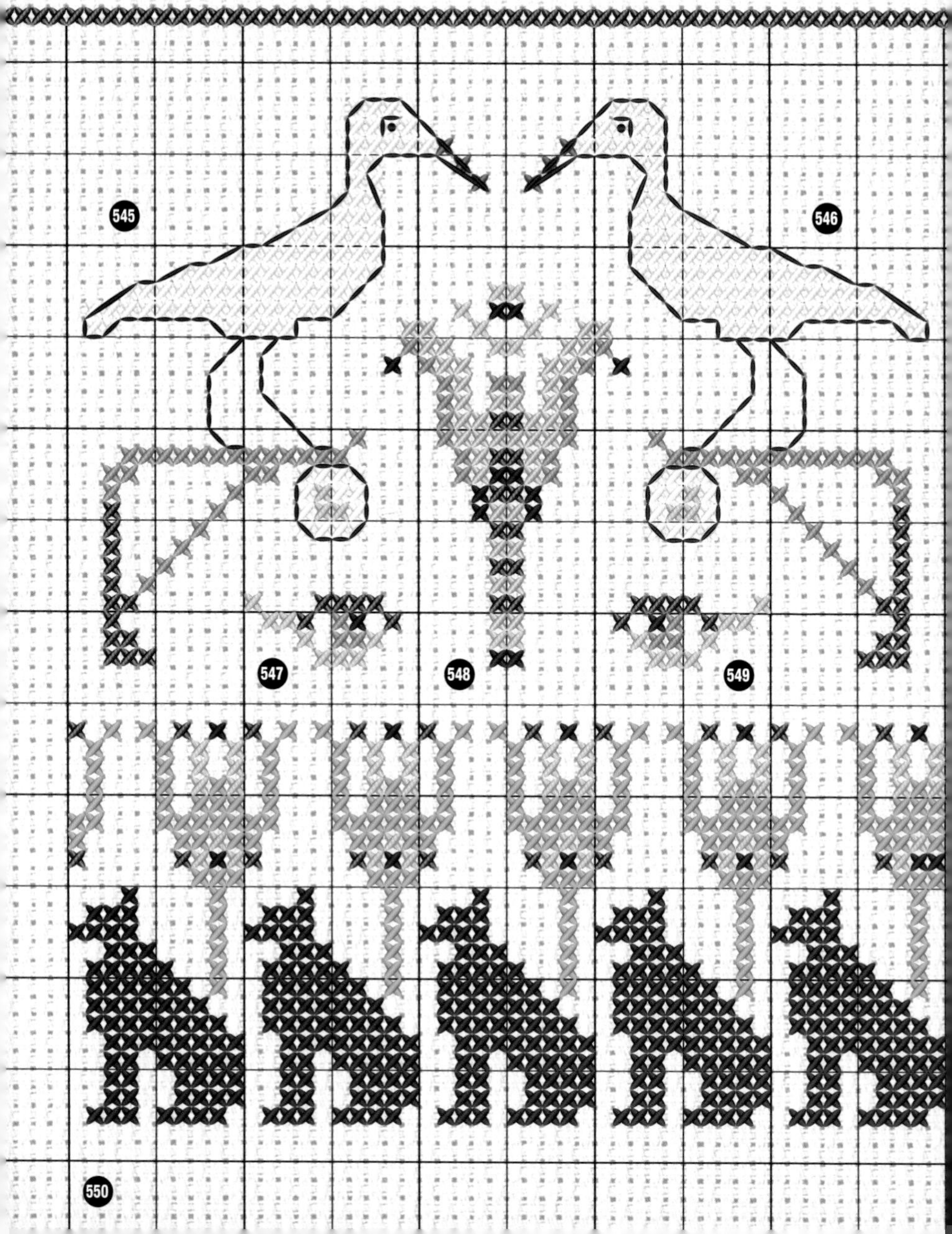

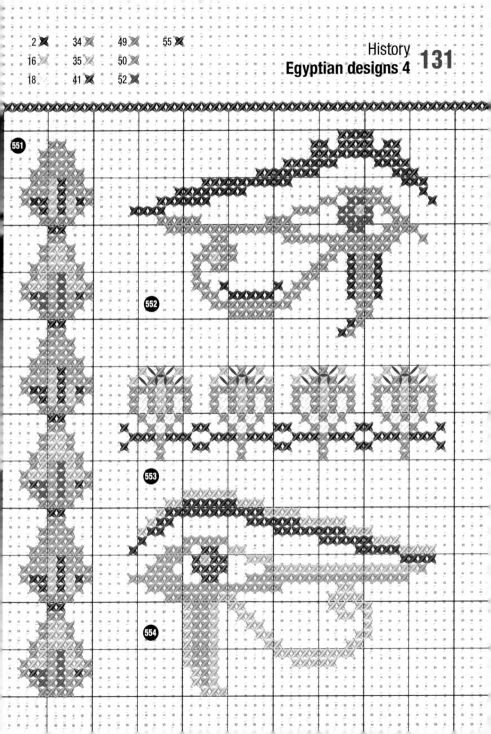

	1		5		14		31
✖	2		9		16		39
	4		12		27		

555

556

557

1 · 11 · 16 · 30 ✖
2 ✖ 13 · 17 · 50 ✖
10 · 15 ✖ 20 ✖ 55 ✖

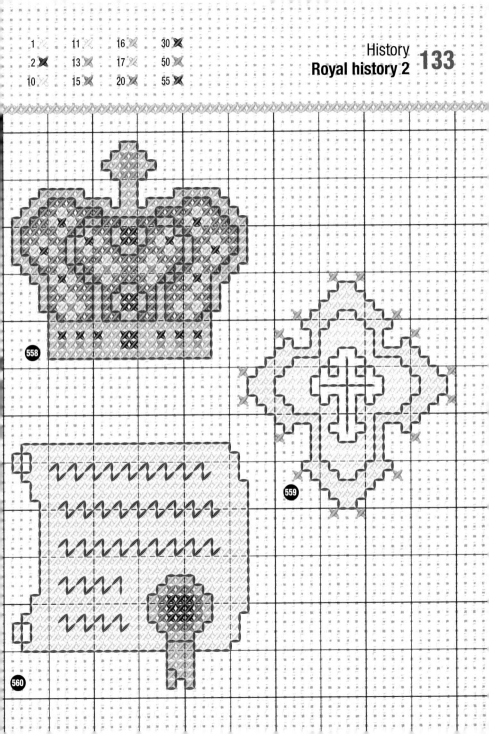

558

559

560

Elizabethan knot gardens 1

17 20 23 31 41 43 47 48 50

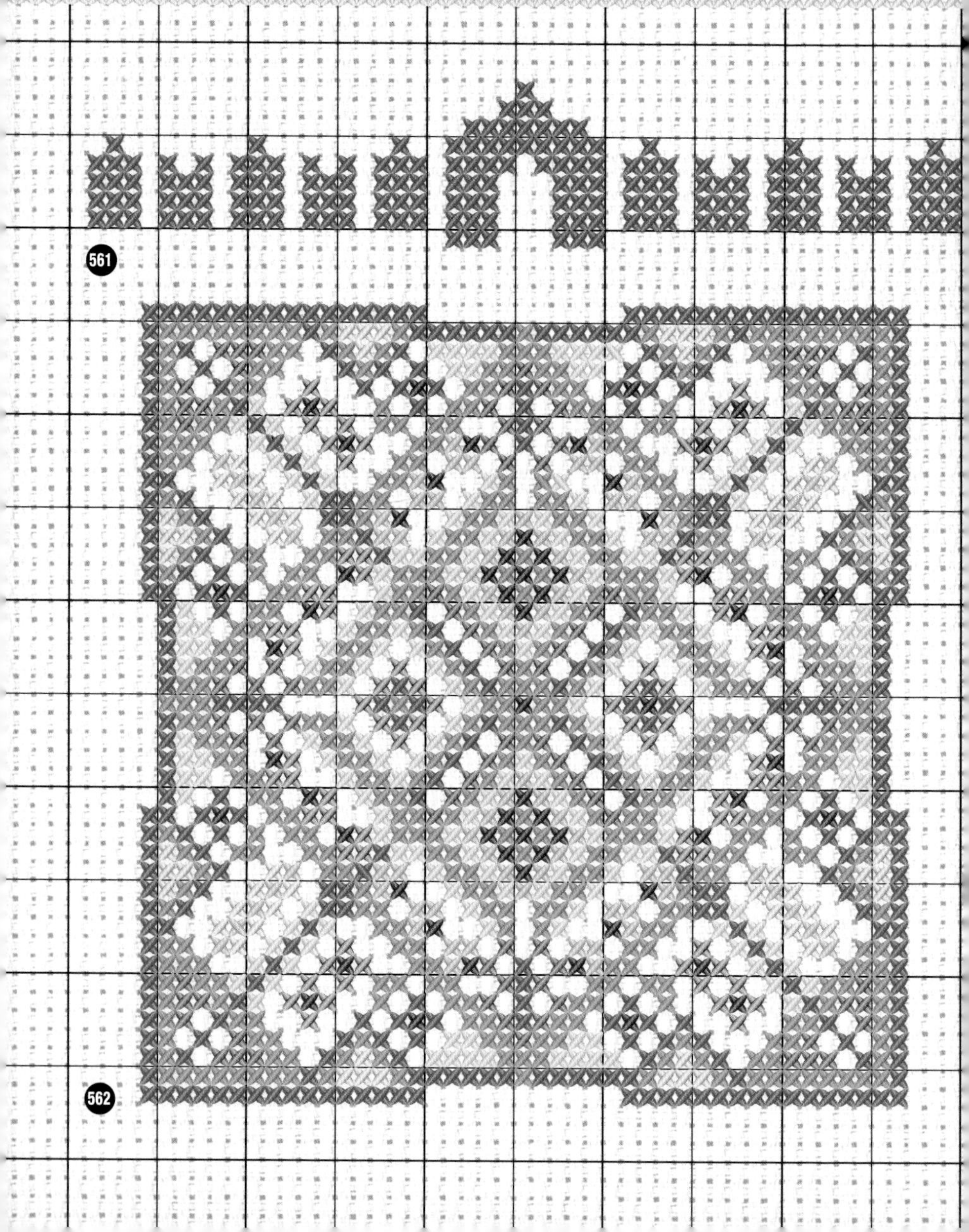

11 ✕ 20 ✕ 47 ✕
17 ✕ 41 ✕ 49 ✕
19 ✕ 43 ✕ 50 ✕

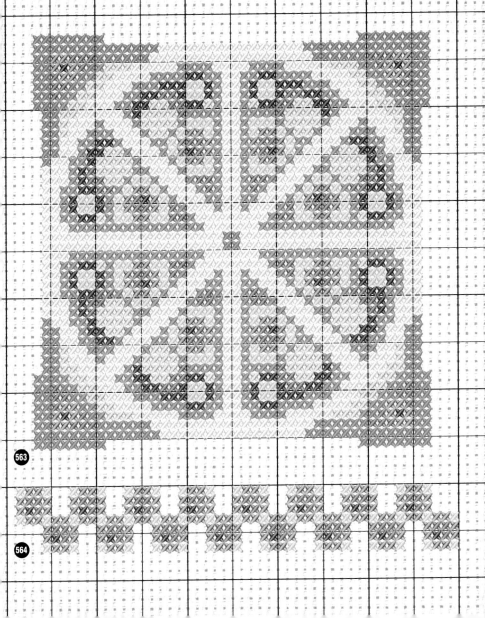

563

564

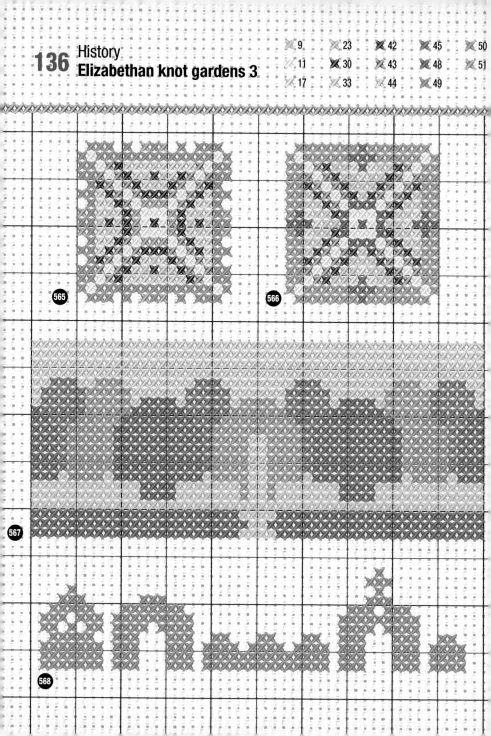

11 19 43 51
14 20 45 52
18 41 49

✖	2	✖	21	✖	24	✖	44	✖	47
✖	19	✖	22	✖	42	✖	45	✖	53
✖	20	✖	23	✖	43	✖	46		

570

571

572

573

574

2 ✖ 18 ✖ 21 ✖ 24 ✖ 47 ✖
16 ✖ 19 ✖ 22 ✖ 45 ✖ 52 ✖
17 ✖ 20 ✖ 23 ✖ 46 ✖ 53 ✖

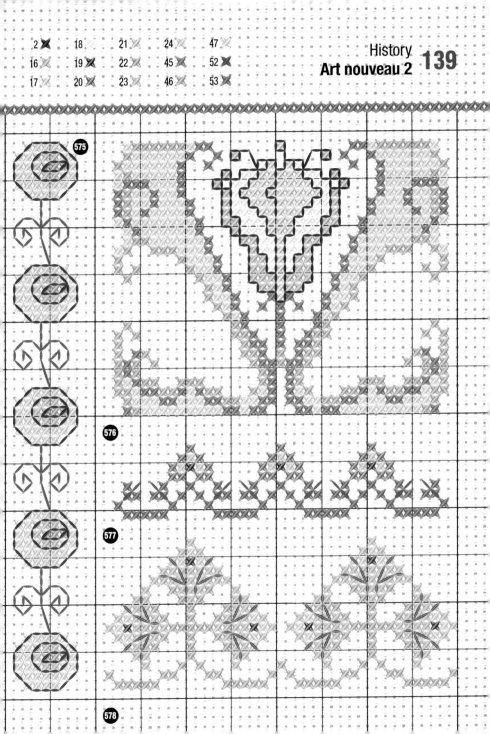

✖ 2		✖ 21		✖ 27		✖ 44		✖ 53
✖ 19		✖ 24		✖ 42		✖ 45		✖ 54
✖ 20		✖ 25		✖ 43		✖ 46		

579

580

581

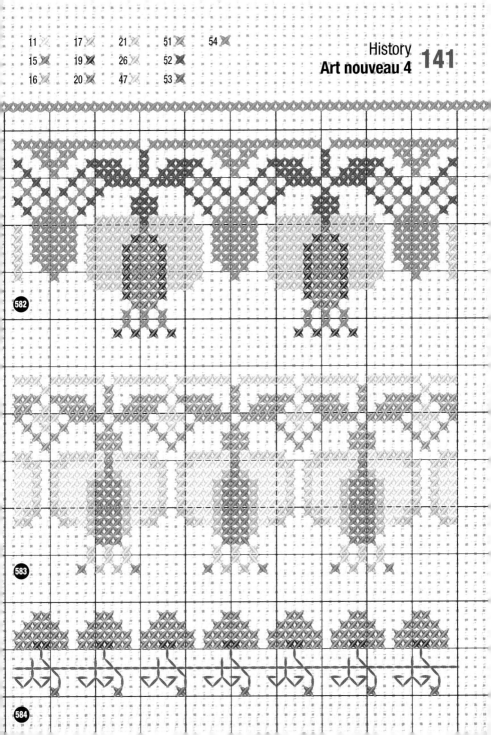

✖ 2	✖ 16	✖ 31
✖ 3	✖ 17	✖ 50
✖ 15	✖ 30	✖ 51

585

586

587

588

589

590

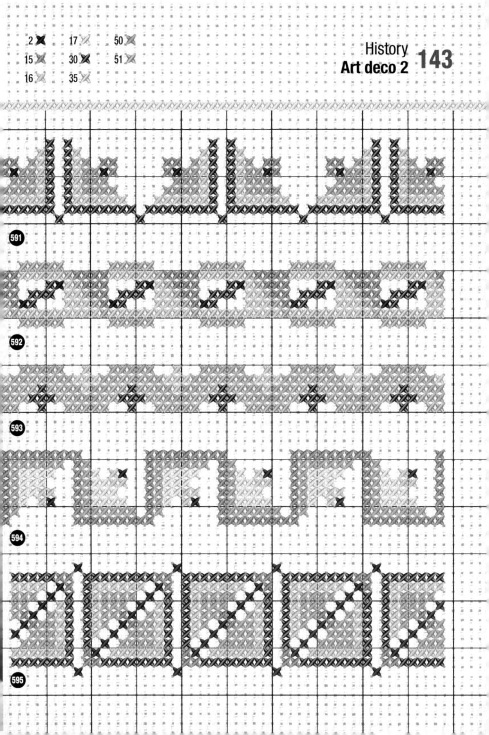

144 History
Art deco 3

2	17	34	51
15	18	35	52
16	30	50	

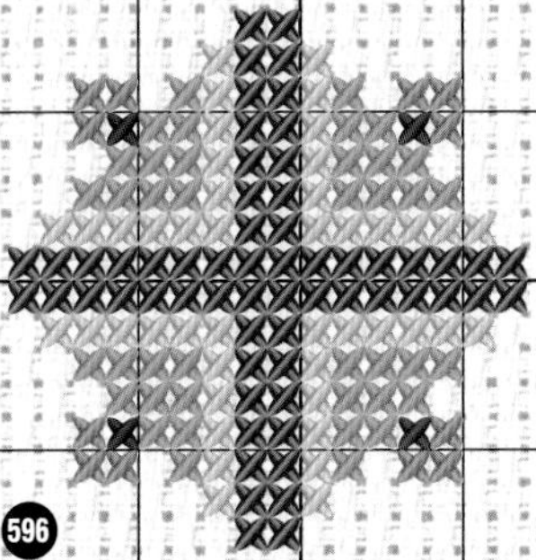

596

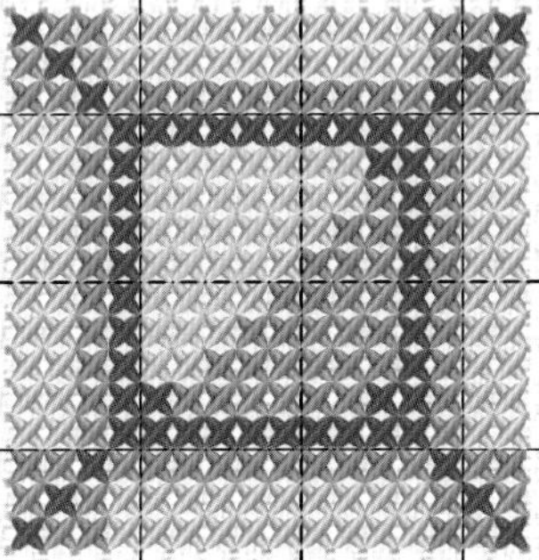

597

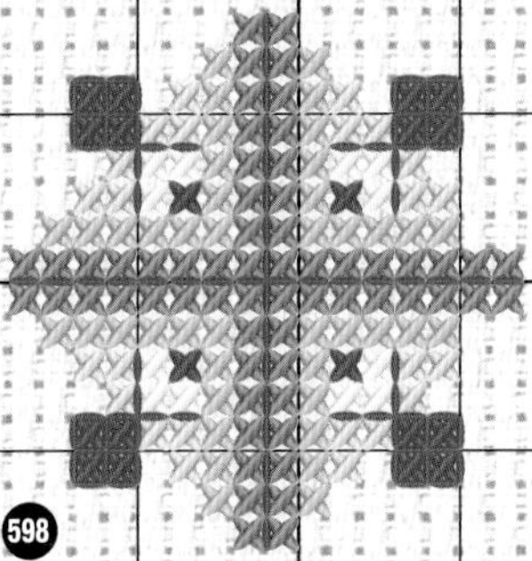

598

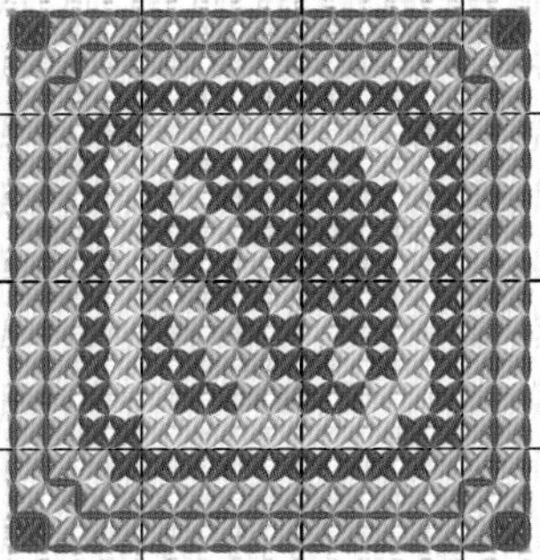

599

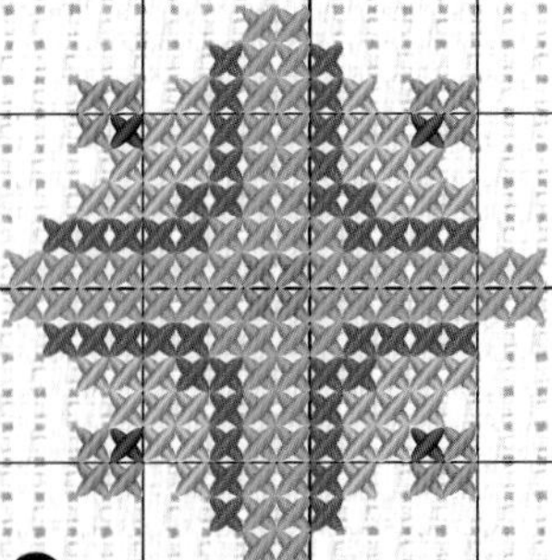

600

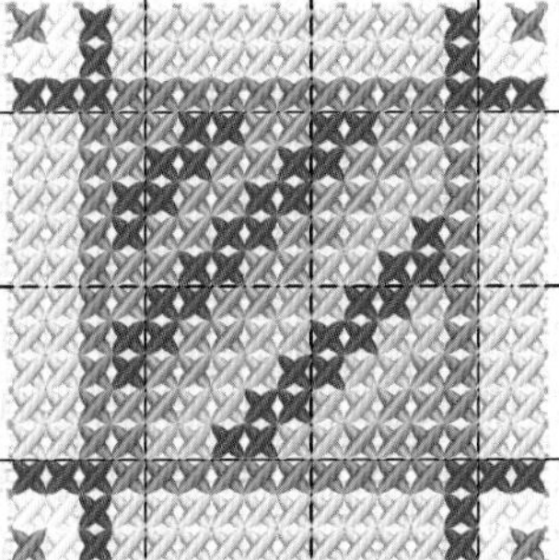

601

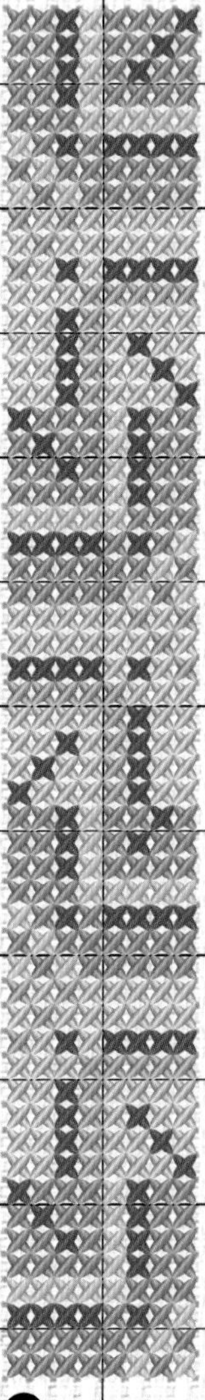

602

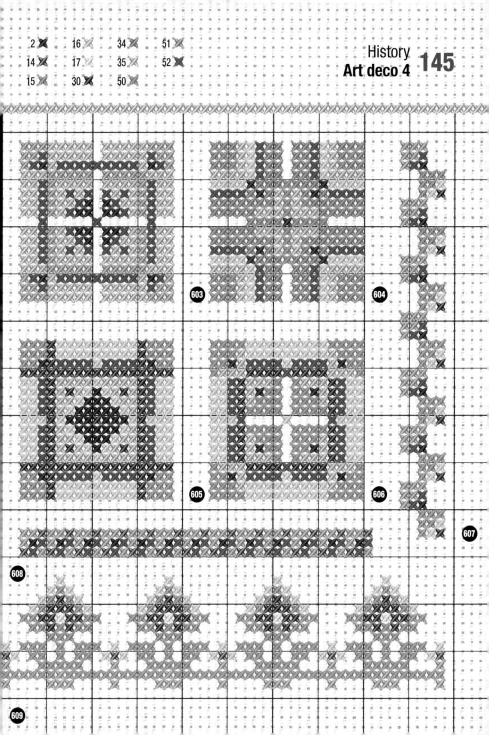

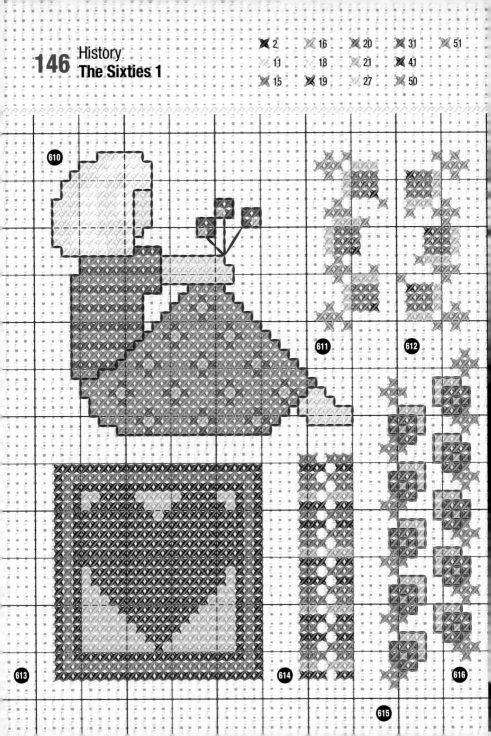

1 7 18 35
2 16 20 504
6 17 32

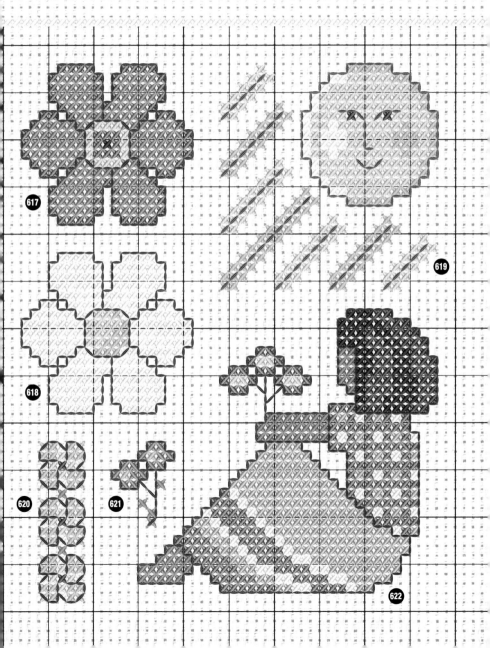

617

618

619

620

621

622

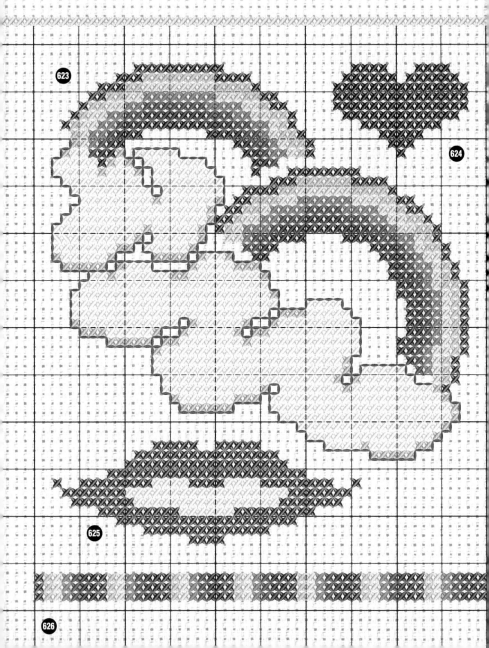

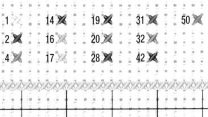

1	14	19	31	50
2	16	20	32	
4	17	28	42	

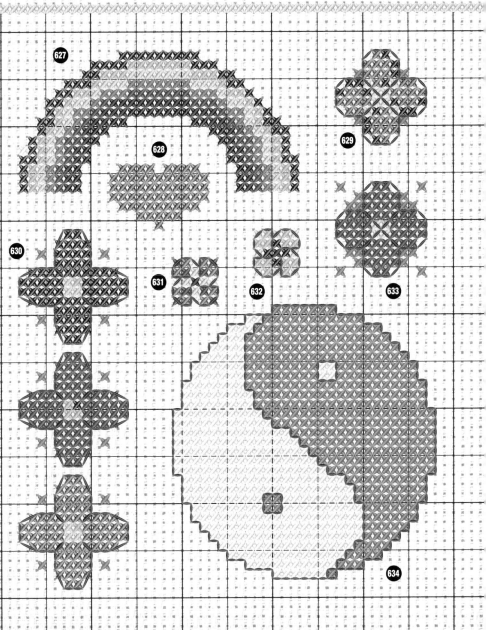

✕ 1	✕ 8	✕ 13	✕ 27
✕ 2	✕ 11	✕ 14	✕ 31
✕ 6	✕ 12	✕ 26	✕ 55

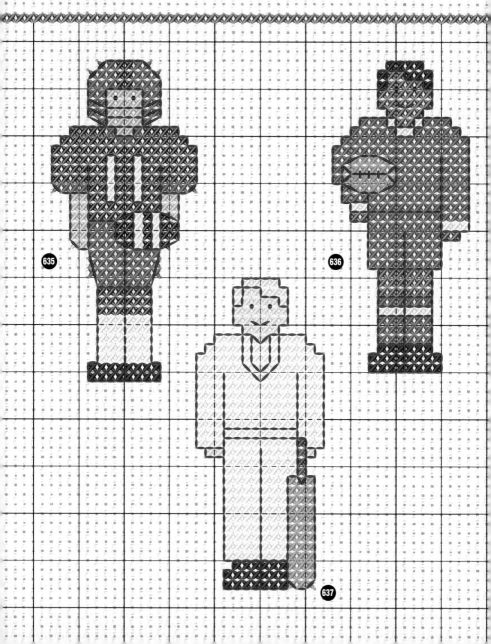

635

636

637

1 ⟋
2 ✖
5 ✖
11 ✖
12 ✖
13 ✖
16 ✖
18
26 ✖
27
31 ✖
35 ✖
55 ✖

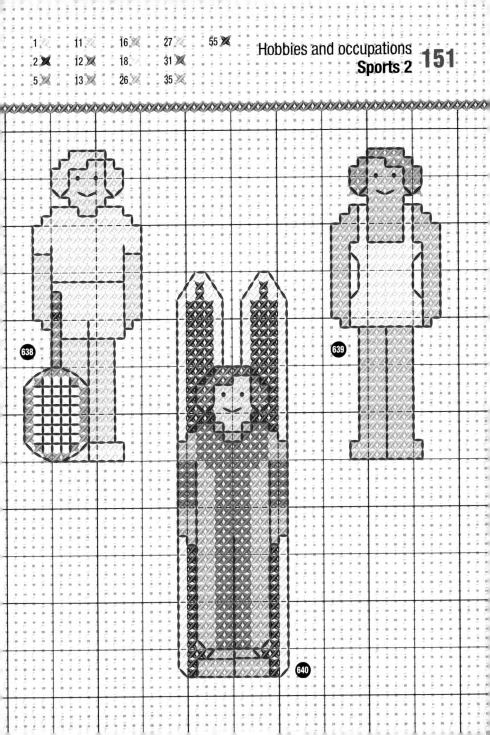

638

639

640

	1		5		12		31
	2		6		26		
	4		7		27		

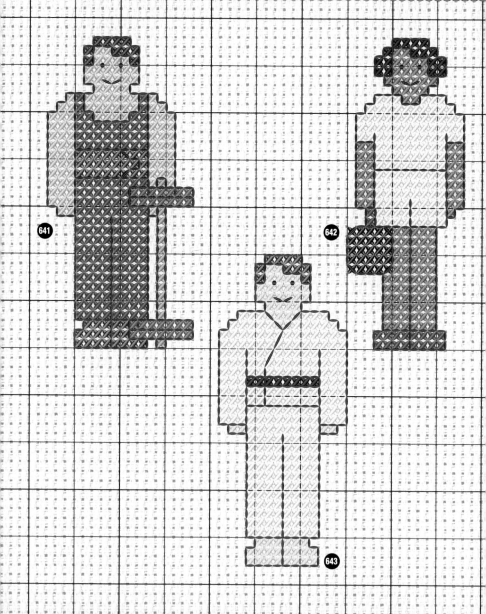

641

642

643

1 · 6 ✖ 13 ✖ 27 ·
2 ✖ 8 ✖ 14 ✖ 30 ✖
5 ✖ 12 ✖ 26 ✖ 50 ✖

644

645

646

✖ 2	✖ 10	✖ 14	✖ 33	✖ 51
✖ 6	✖ 11	✖ 21	✖ 37	✖ 56
1	✖ 8	✖ 13	✖ 31	✖ 47	✖ 57

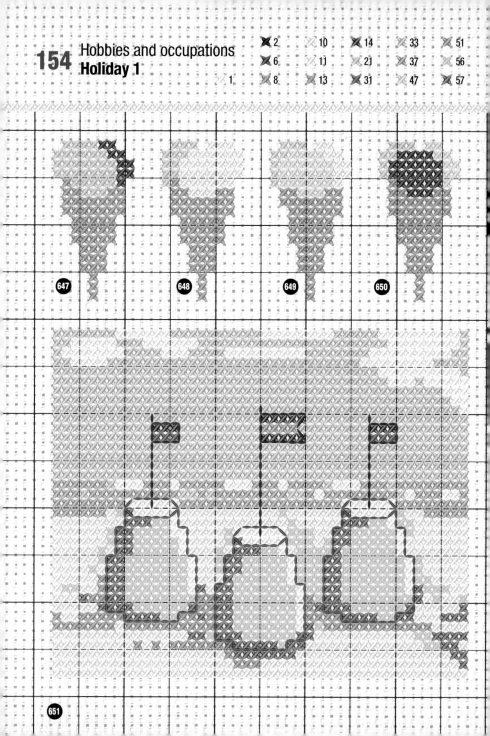

647
648
649
650

651

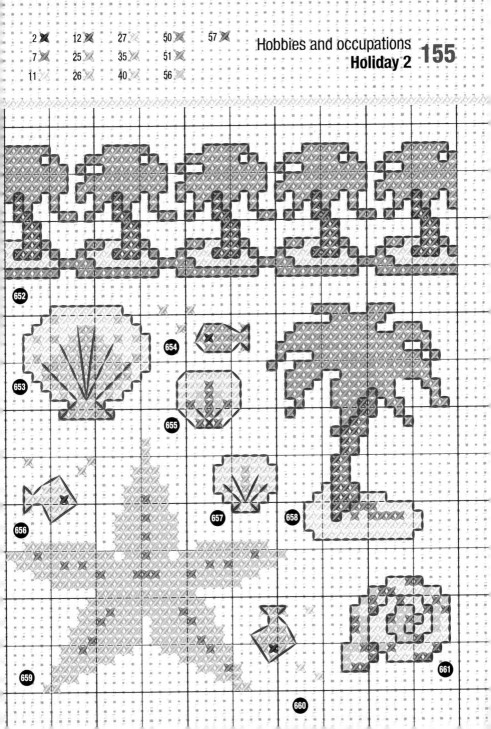

2 ✖ 12 ✖ 27 ✖ 50 ✖ 57 ✖
7 ✖ 25 ✖ 35 ✖ 51 ✖
11 26 ✖ 40 ✖ 56 ✖

652

653

654

655

656

657

658

659

660

661

✖ 2	✖ 8	✖ 11	✖ 31	✖ 57
✖ 4	✖ 9	✖ 14	✖ 33	
✖ 7	✖ 10	✖ 16	✖ 56	

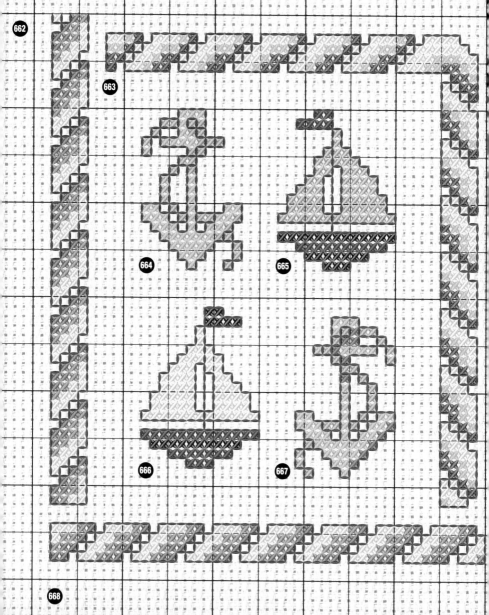

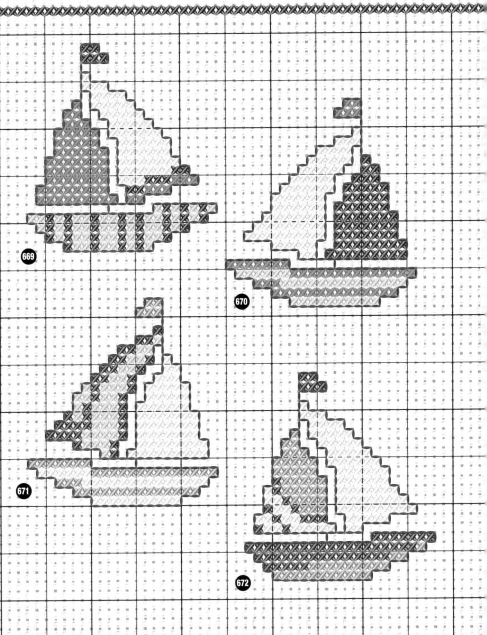

╳ 1	✖ 6	✖ 12	✖ 28
✖ 2	✖ 7	✖ 13	╳ 40
✖ 3	╳ 11	╳ 27	

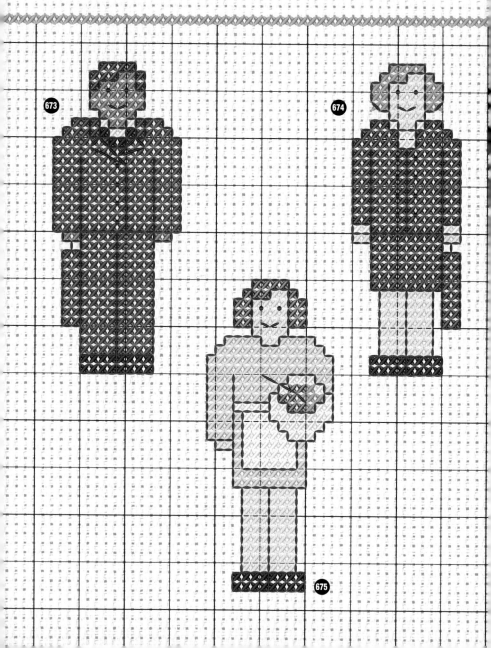

673
674
675

1   11   16   27   43
2   13   17   29   50
8   14   26   32

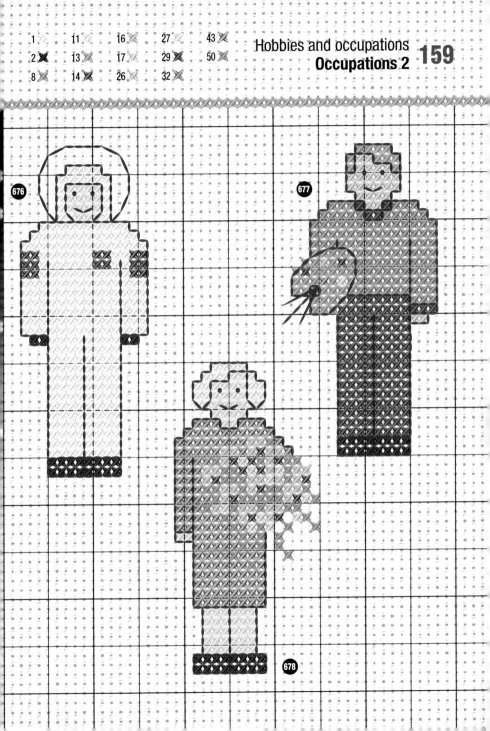

676

677

678

1	11	26	37
2	12	27	38
5	13	29	55

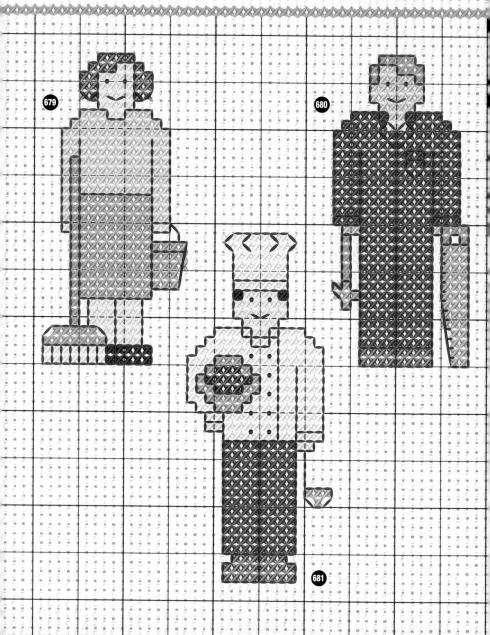

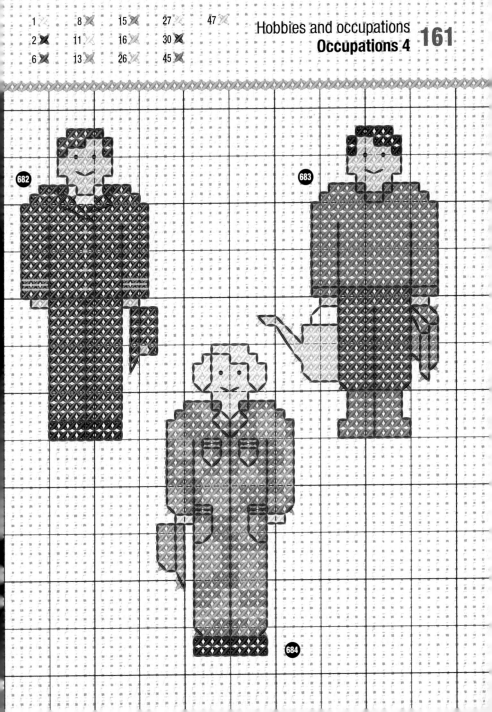

✖ 2	✖ 11	✖ 31	✖ 55
✖ 4	✖ 14	✖ 32	
✖ 8	✖ 17	✖ 50	

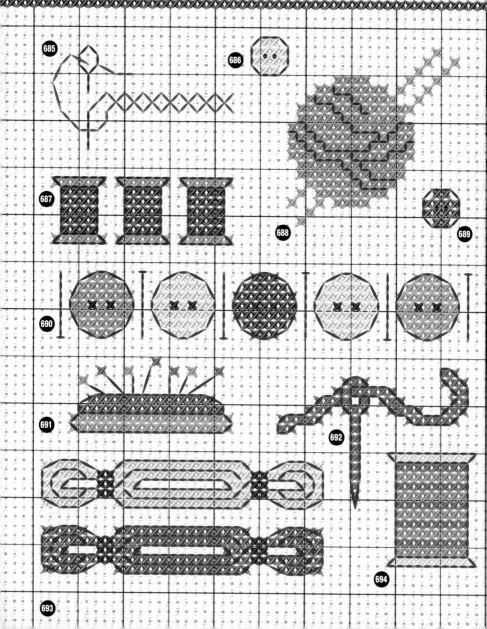

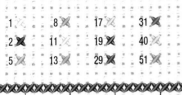

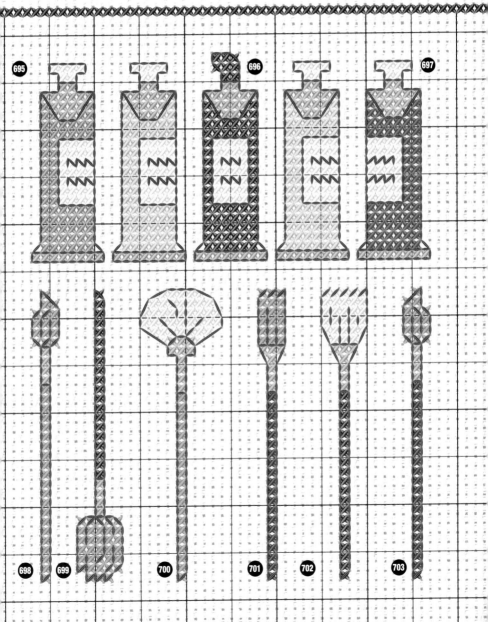

✖ 2		✖ 13		✖ 21		✖ 31		✖ 56	
✖ 4		✖ 15		✖ 22		✖ 50		✖ 57	
✖ 5		✖ 17		✖ 30		✖ 51			

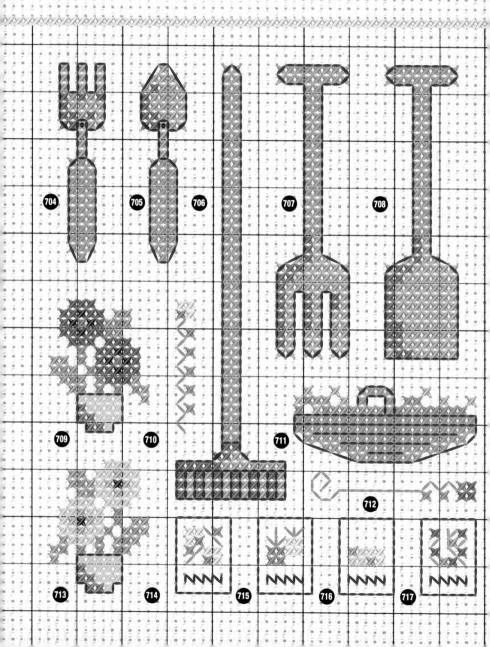

2 ✖   21 ✖   47 ✖   52 ✖   56 ✖
17 ✖   45 ✖   48 ✖   53 ✖   57 ✖
20 ✖   467 ✖   49 ✖   54 ✖

Hobbies and occupations
Hobbies 4 165

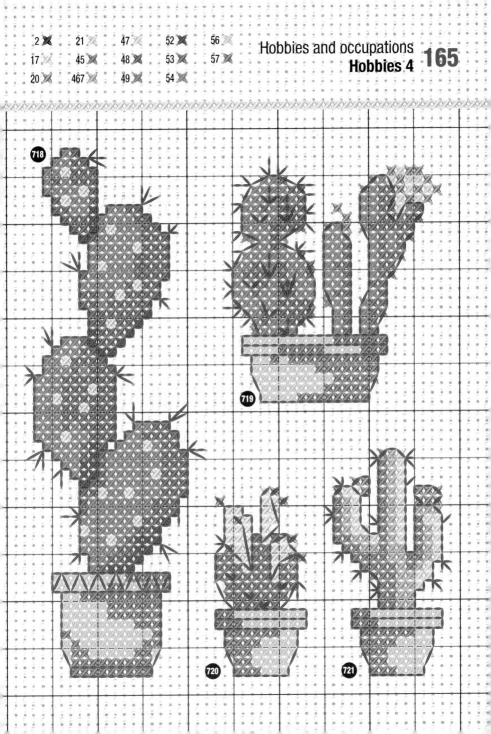

166 Hobbies and occupations
Zodiac symbols 1

34

35

722
723
724
725
726
727

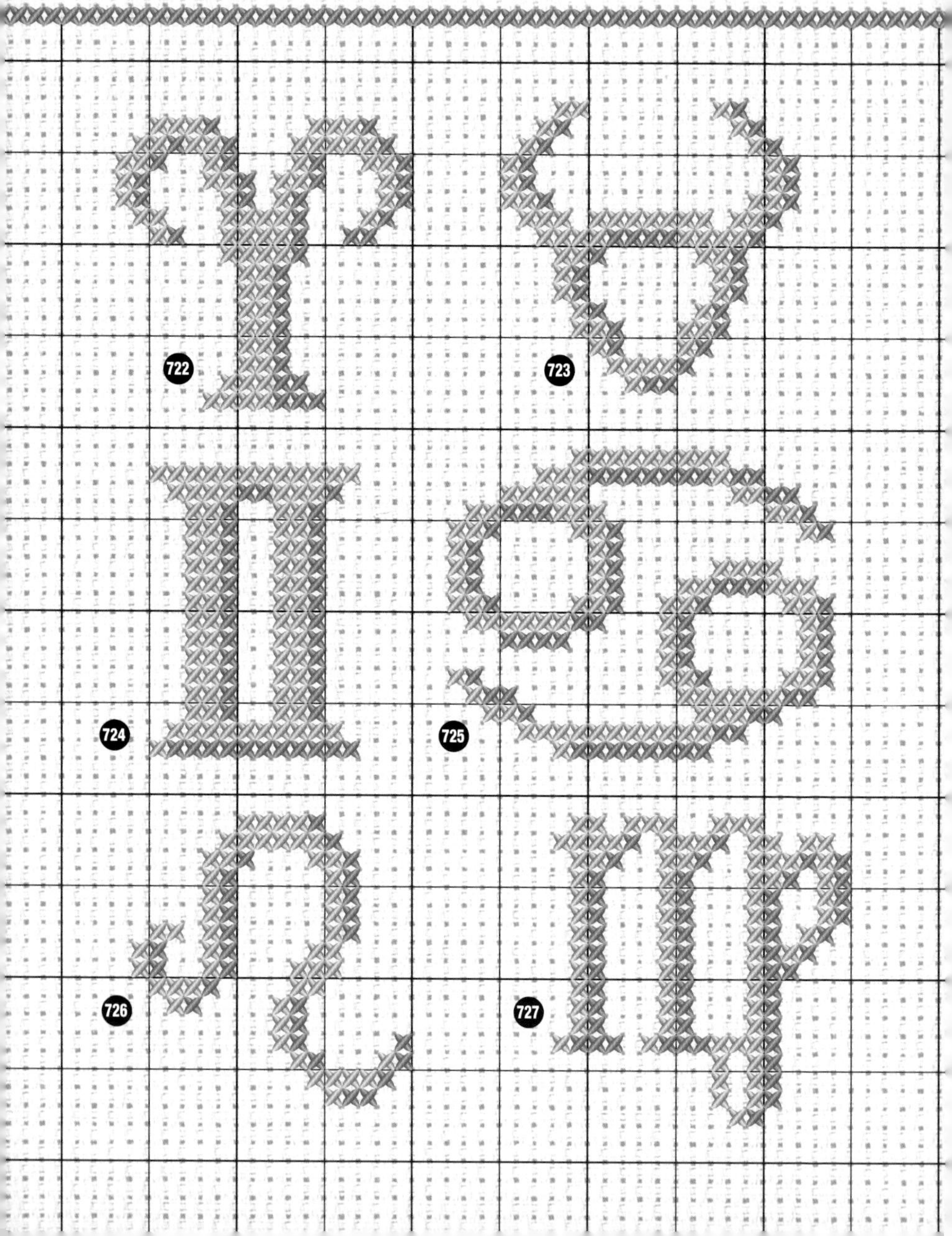

34
35

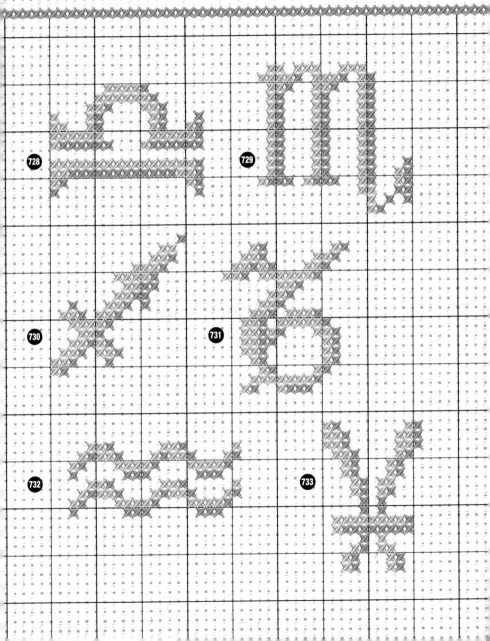

2 ✖   17 ✖
13 ✖   31 ✖
14 ✖   50 ✖

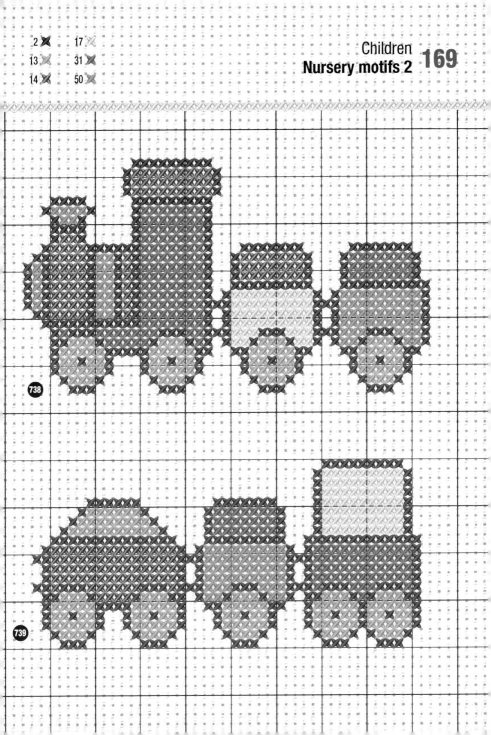

738

739

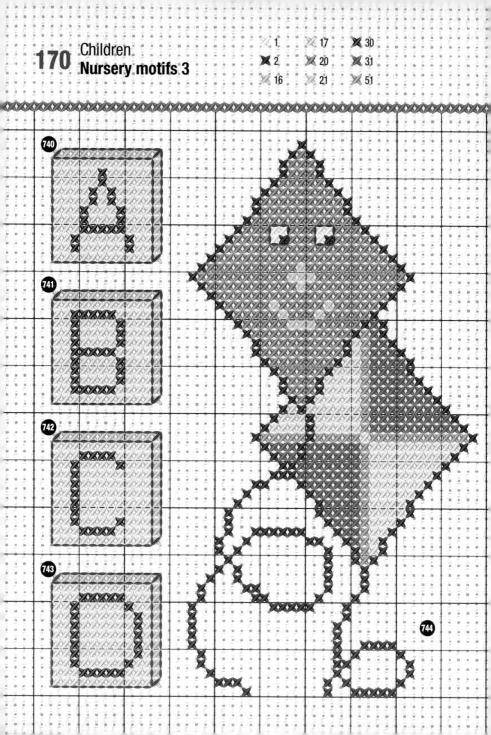

2 ✖ 17 ✖ 40 ✖
14 ✖ 31 ✖
16 ✖ 33 ✖

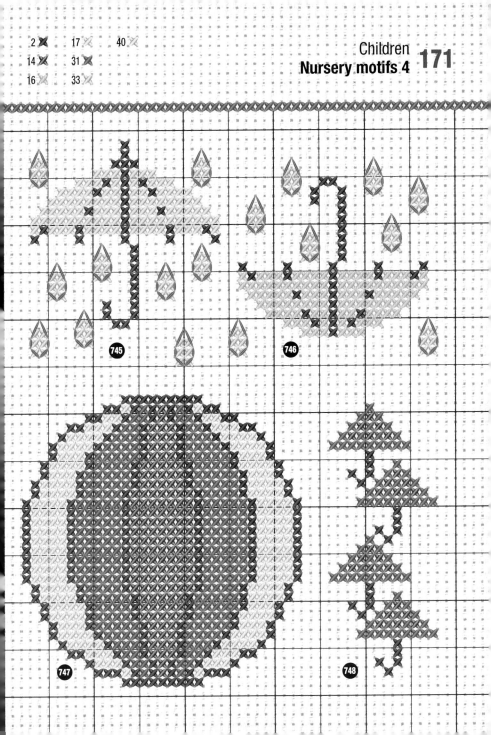

745

746

747

748

1		10		30	
2		14		49	
4		17		55	

749

750

751

752

753

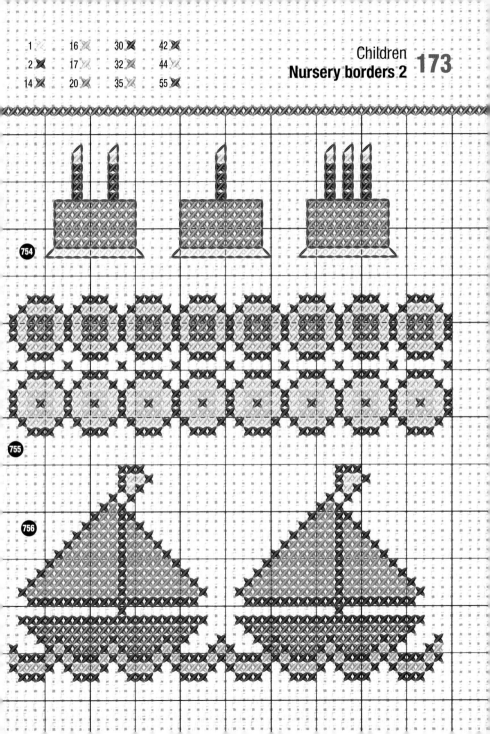

1   8   31   49
2   14   35   50
6   17   40

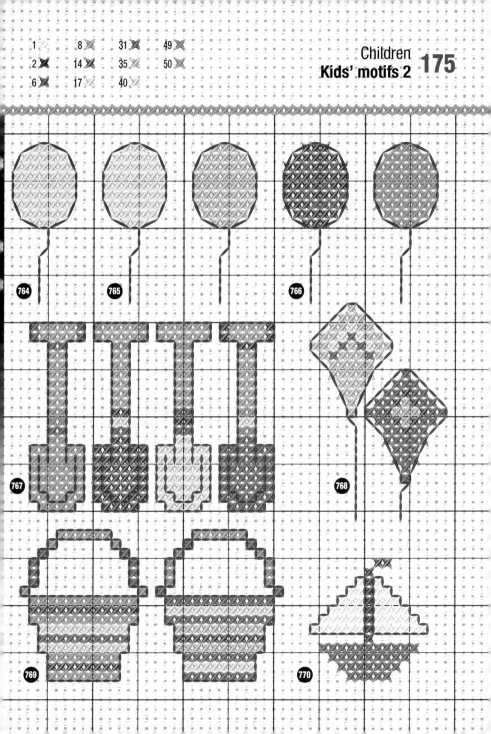

764   765   766

767   768

769   770

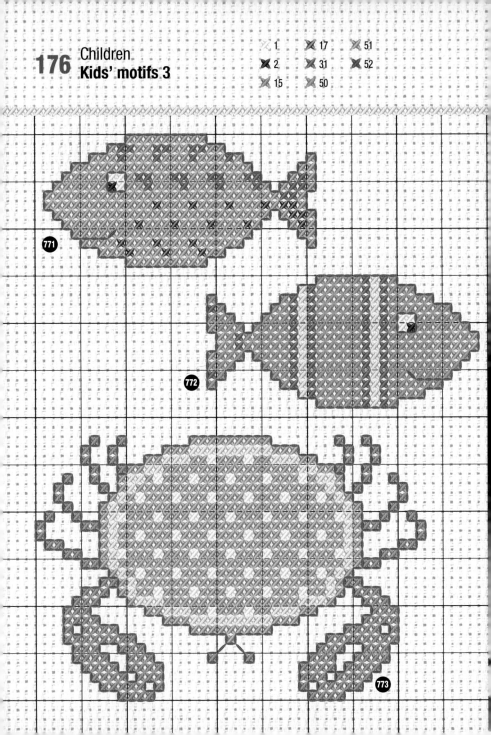

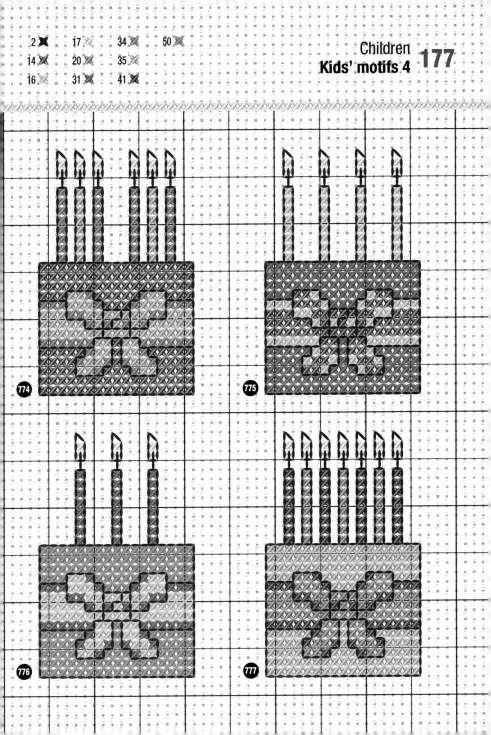

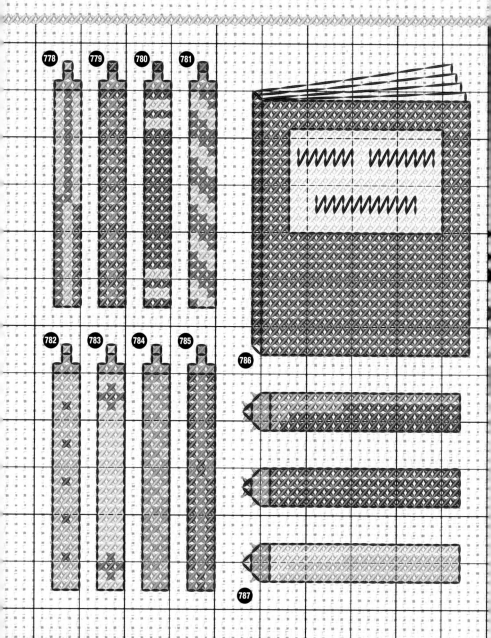

☒ 1	☒ 14	☒ 31	☒ 41	☒ 50
☒ 2	☒ 16	☒ 35	☒ 43	☒ 55
☒ 13	☒ 17	☒ 40	☒ 49	

778 779 780 781 786

782 783 784 785 787

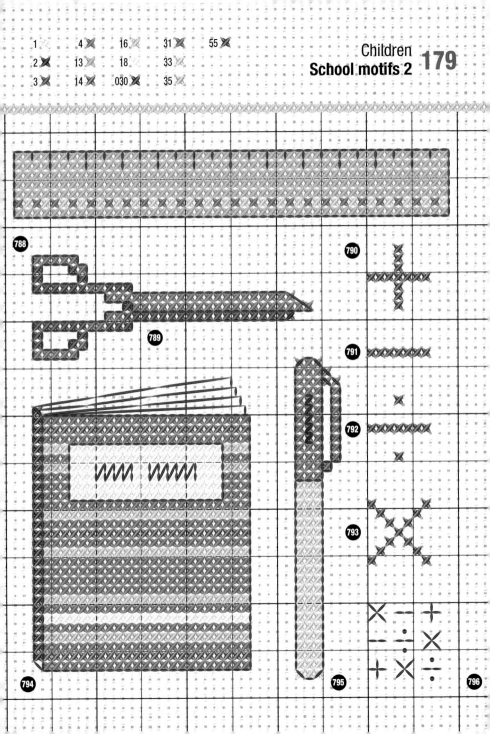

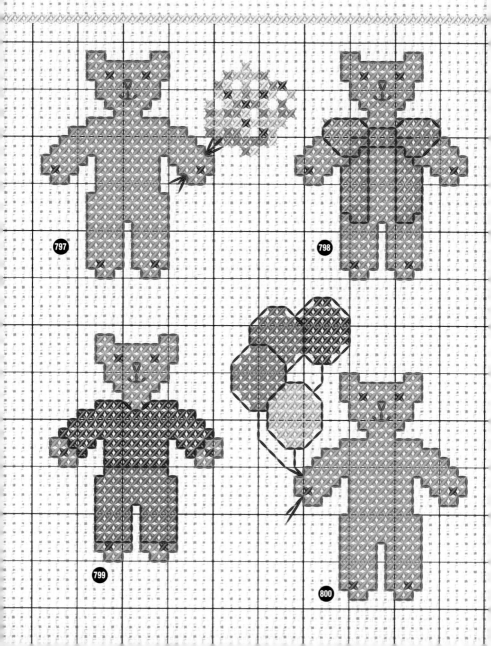

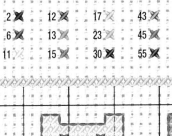

✖ 2	✖ 12	18	✖ 51
✖ 6	✖ 13	26	
11	✖ 14	✖ 31	

804

805

806

807

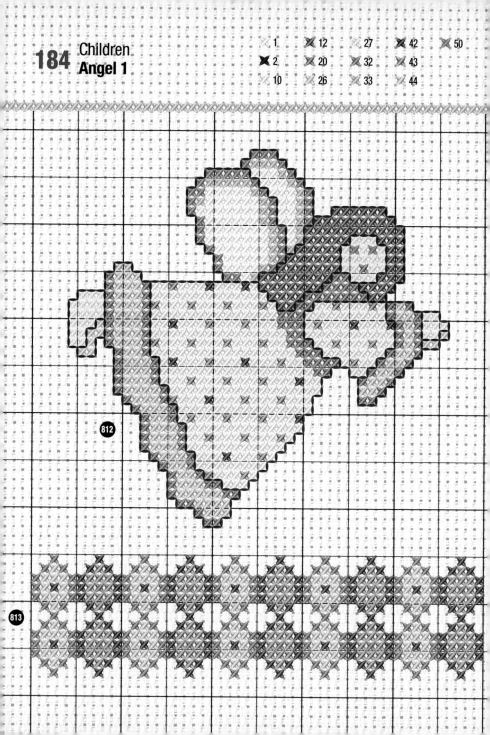

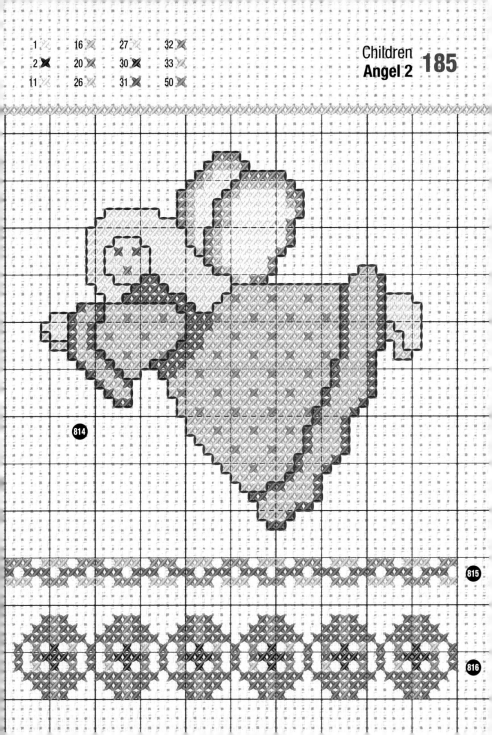

186 Geometric
Narrow bands 1

7
12
8
13
11
16

817
818
819
820
821
822
823
824

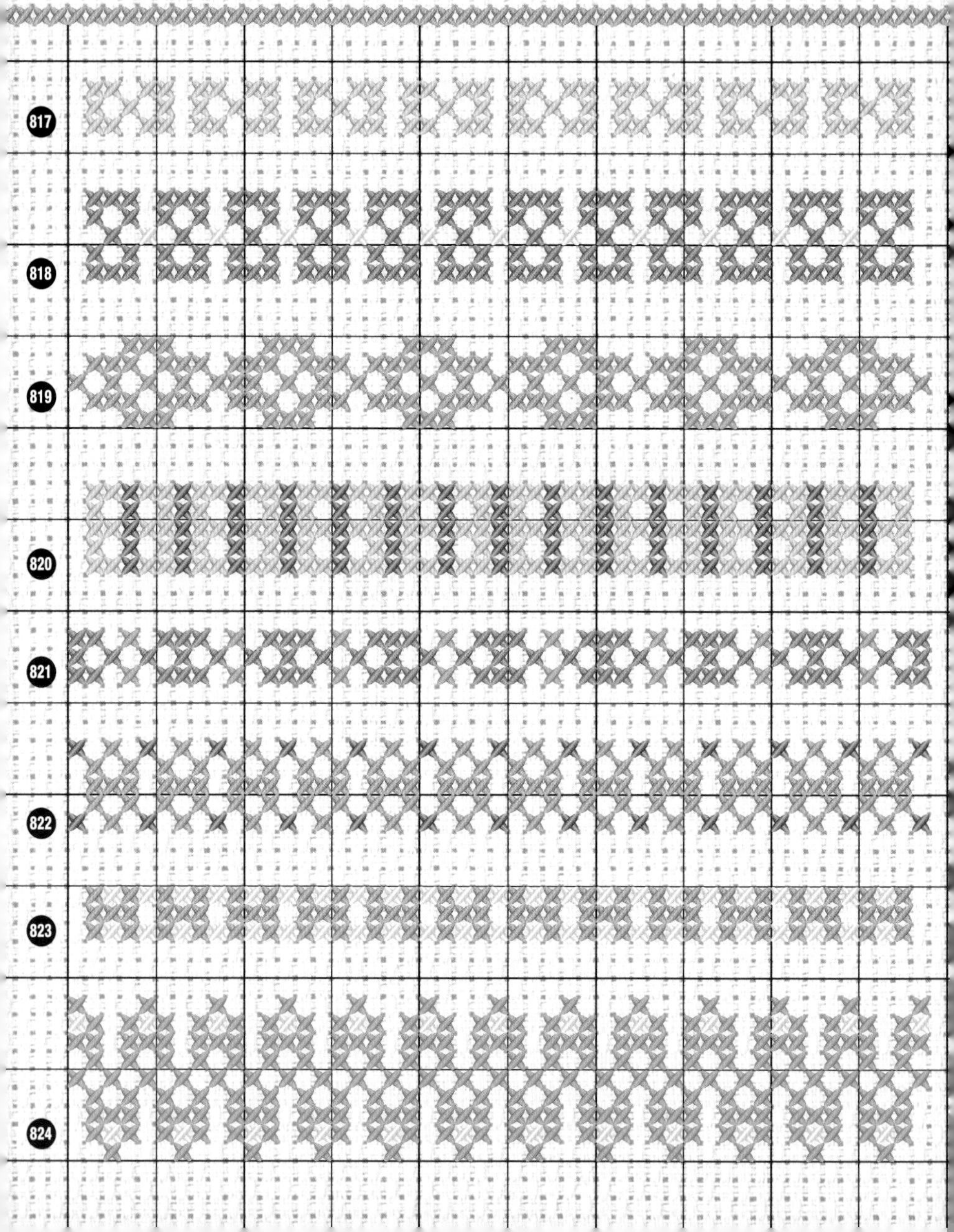

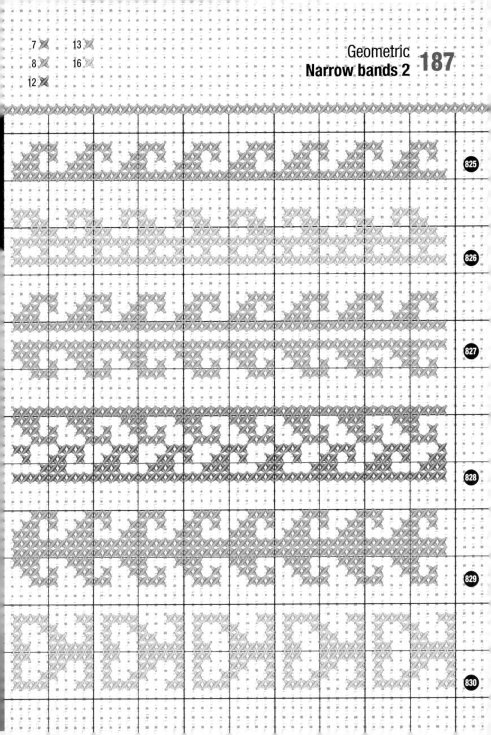

Geometric
Narrow bands 3

✖ 30	✖ 33	✖ 41
✖ 31	✖ 36	✖ 43
✖ 32	✖ 37	

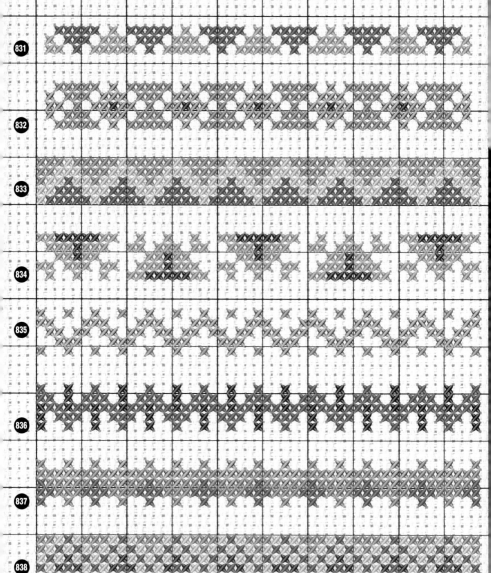

831

832

833

834

835

836

837

838

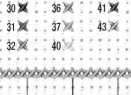

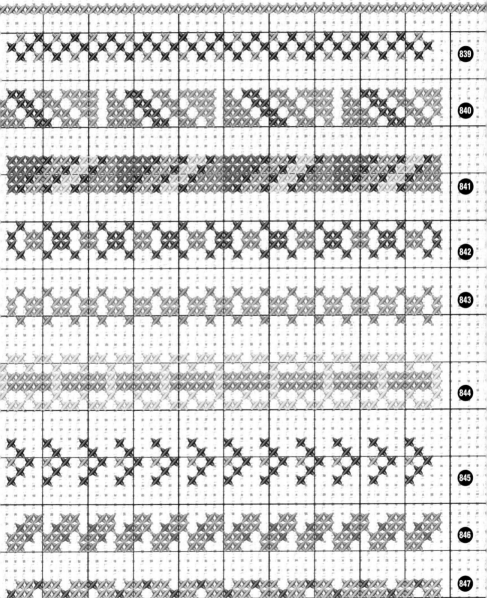

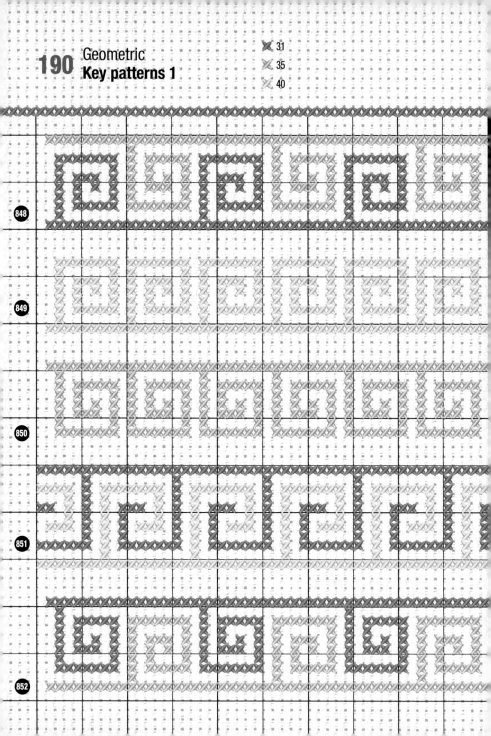

31
35
40

848

849

850

851

852

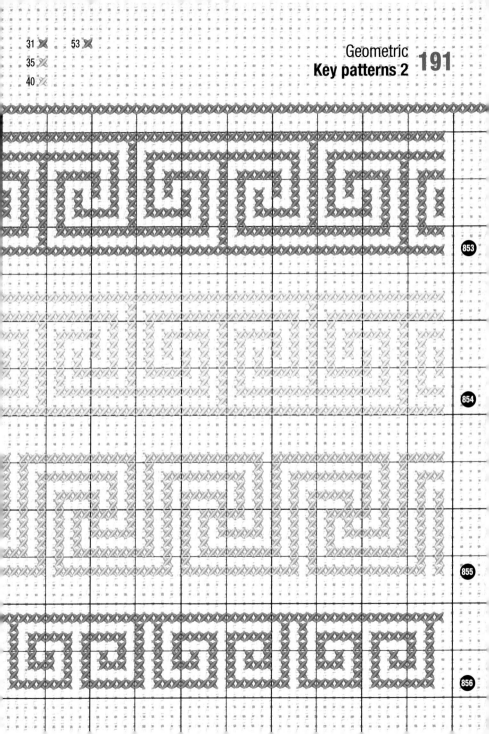

Repeat patterns 1

19 22
20 23
21 25

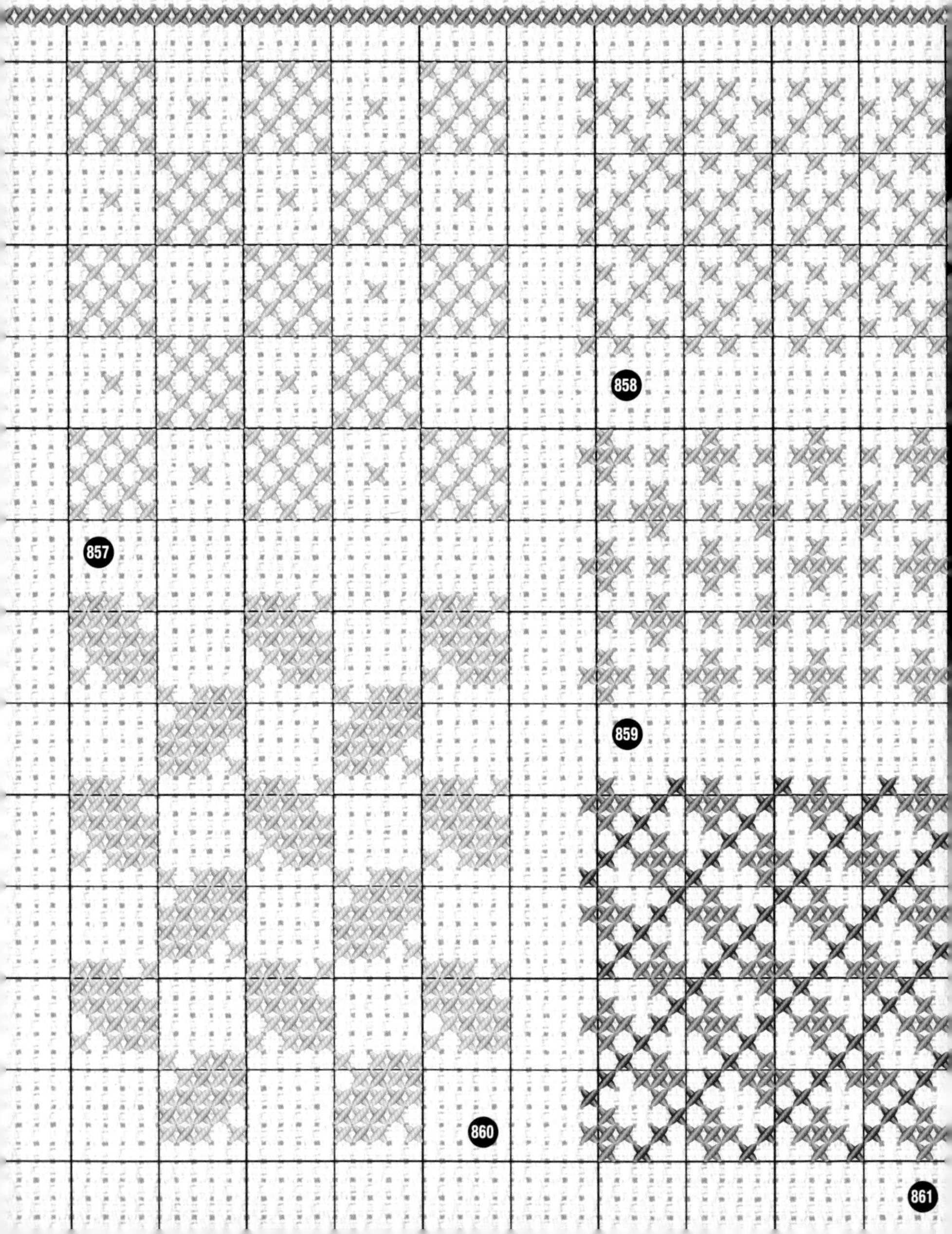
857
858
859
860
861

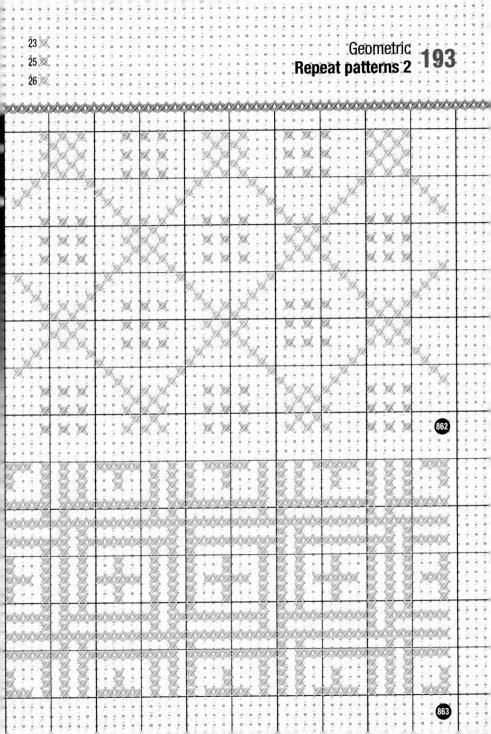

X 6   X 11   X 16
X 7   X 12
X 8   X 13

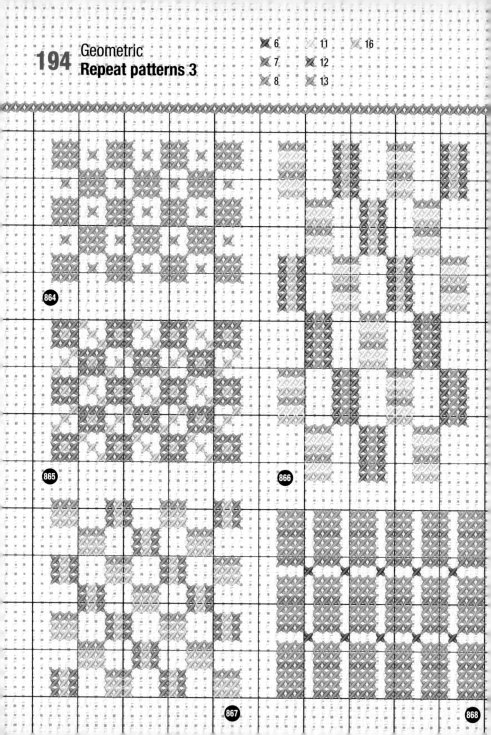

864

865

866

867

868

6 ✕ 9 ✕ 13 ✕
7 ✕ 11 ✕ 15 ✕
8 ✕ 12 ✕ 16 ✕

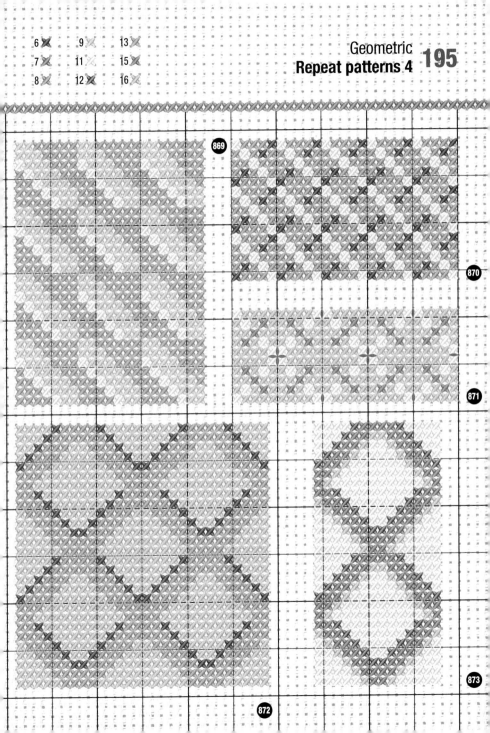

869

870

871

872

873

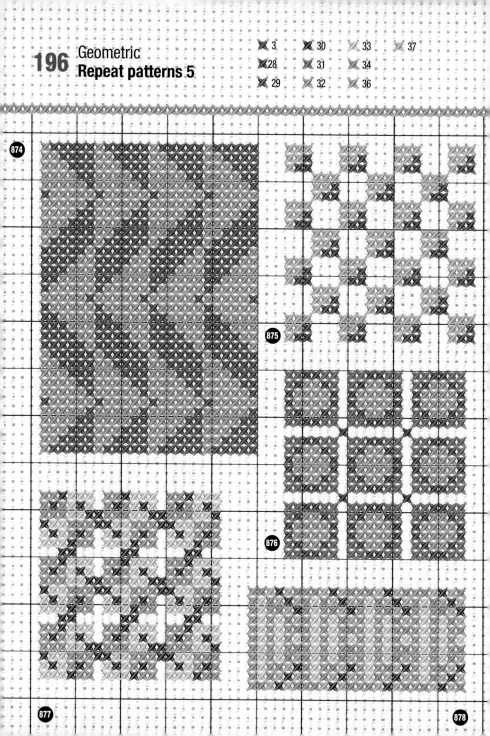

3 ✖   32 ✖   37 ✖   43 ✖
28 ✖   33 ✖   38 ✖   44 ✖
31 ✖   36 ✖   41 ✖

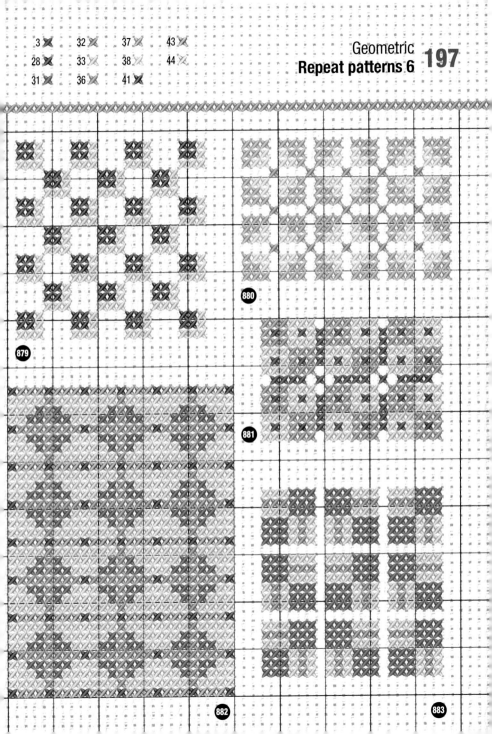

879

880

881

882

883

Color key:
- ✕ 2
- ✕ 39
- ✕ 40
- ✕ 46
- ✕ 47
- ✕ 48
- ✕ 49
- ✕ 50
- ✕ 51
- ✕ 53
- ✕ 54

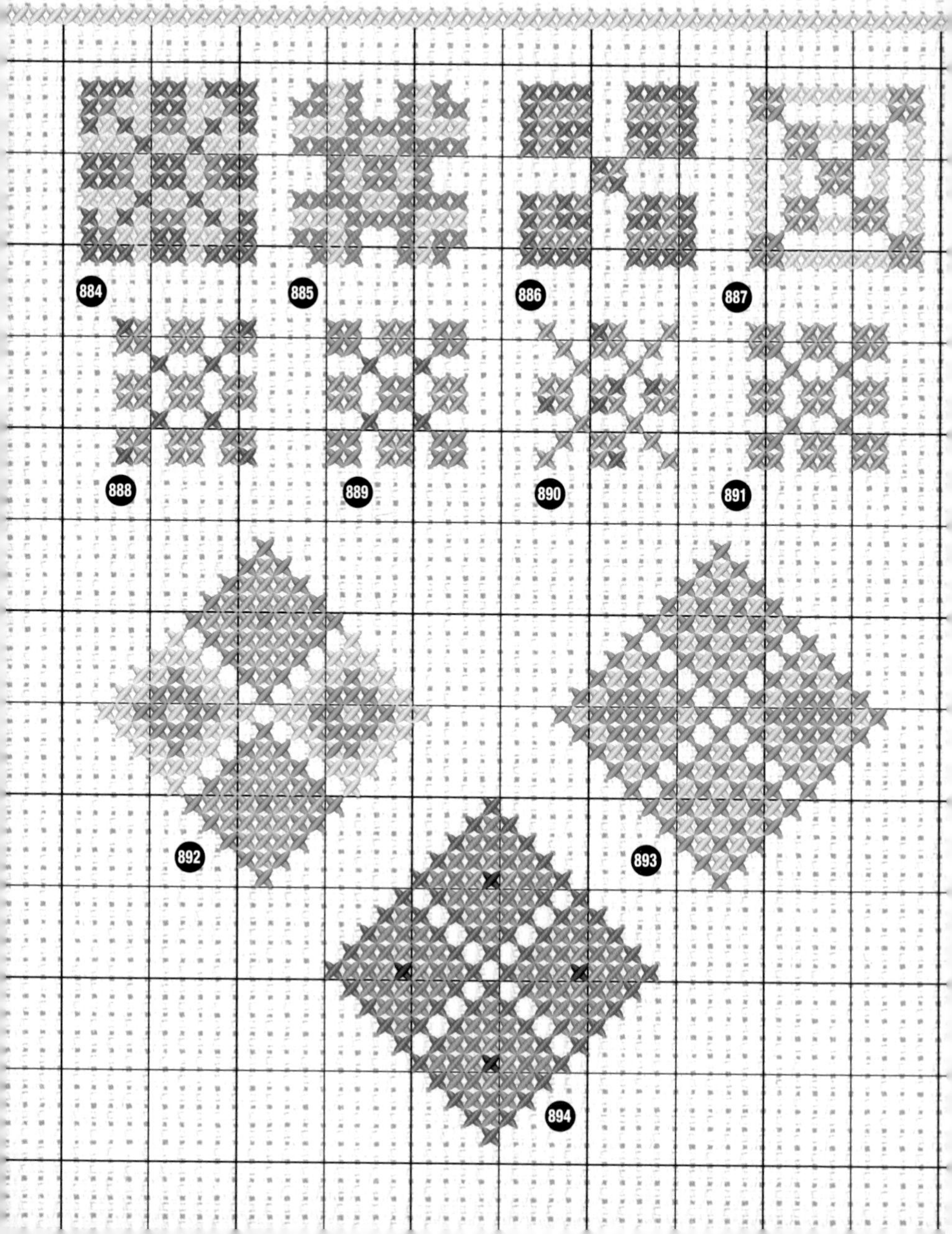

884 885 886 887

888 889 890 891

892 893

894

2 ✖ 45 ✖ 48 ✖ 53 ✖
39 ✖ 46 ✖ 50 ✖ 54 ✖
40 ✖ 47 ✖ 51 ✖

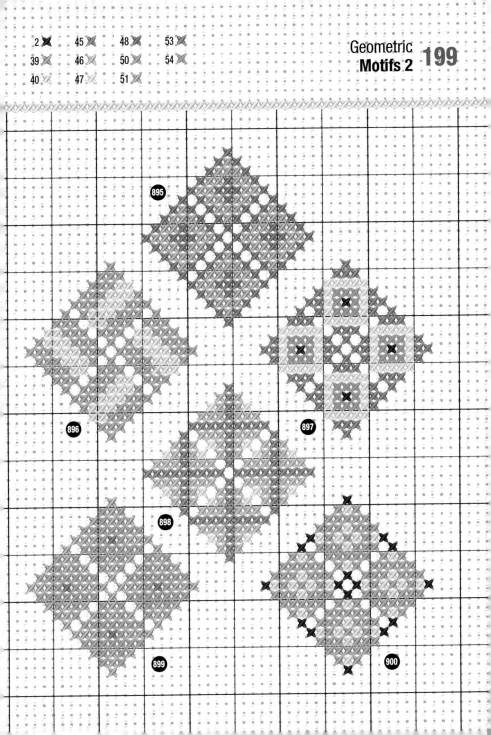

Geometric

Knot patterns 1

21 32 43
23 33 44
24 38

901

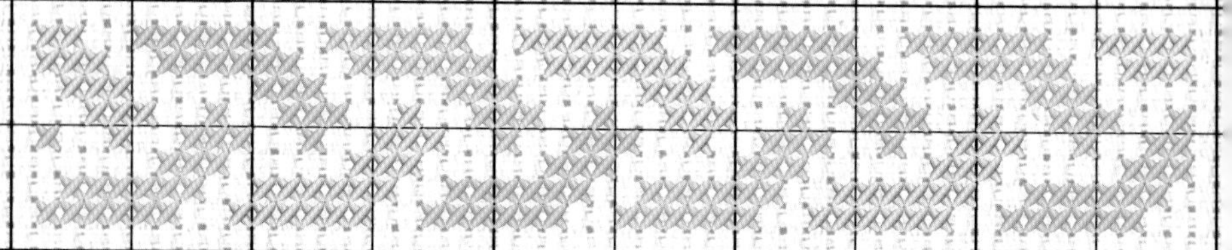

902

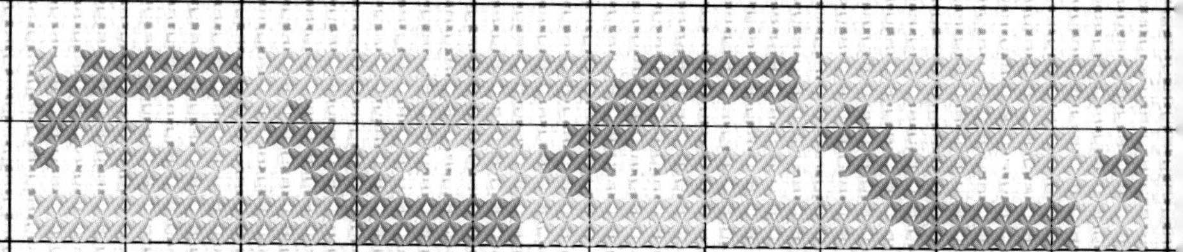

903

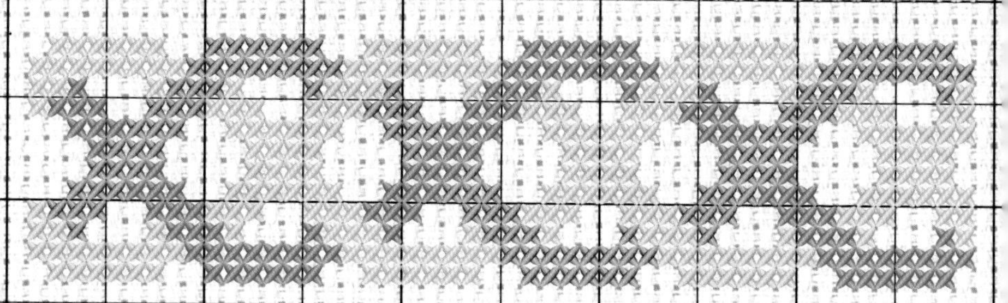

904

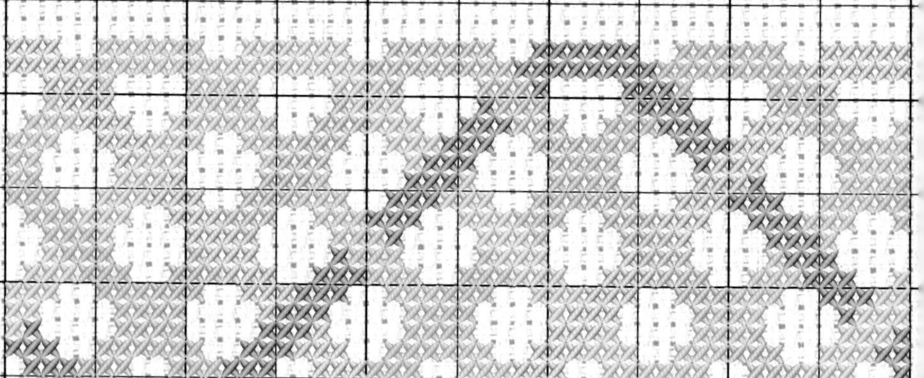

3 ✕   26 ✕   38 ✕
21 ✕   32 ✕   43 ✕
23 ✕   33 ✕   44 ✕

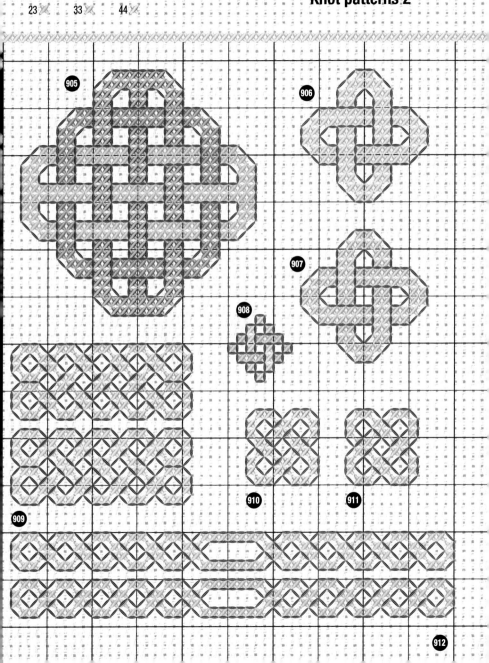

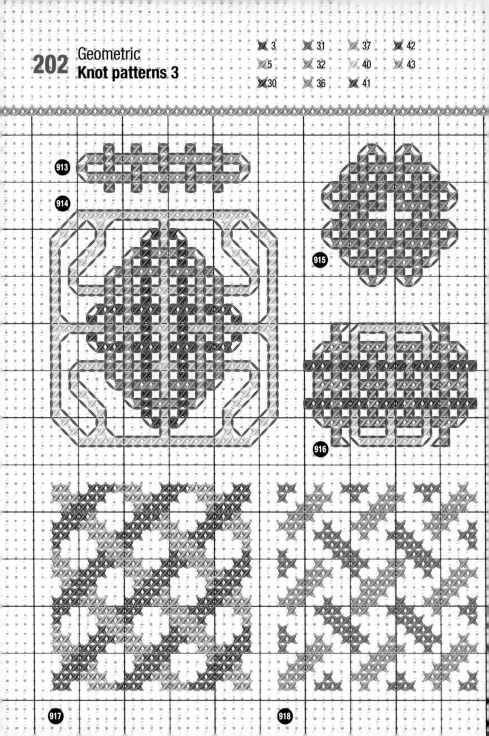

3 ✖   40 ✖
31 ✖
32 ✖

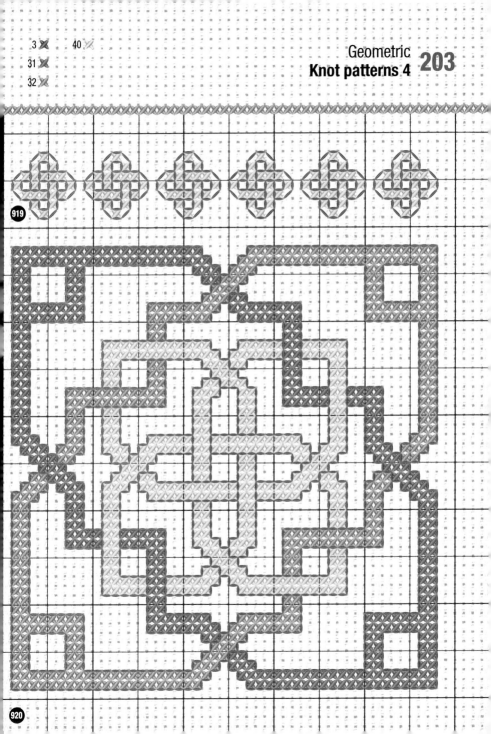

919

920

✕ 3	✕ 21	✕ 25
✕ 19	✕ 22	✕ 42
✕ 20	✕ 24	

921
922
923 924
925 926

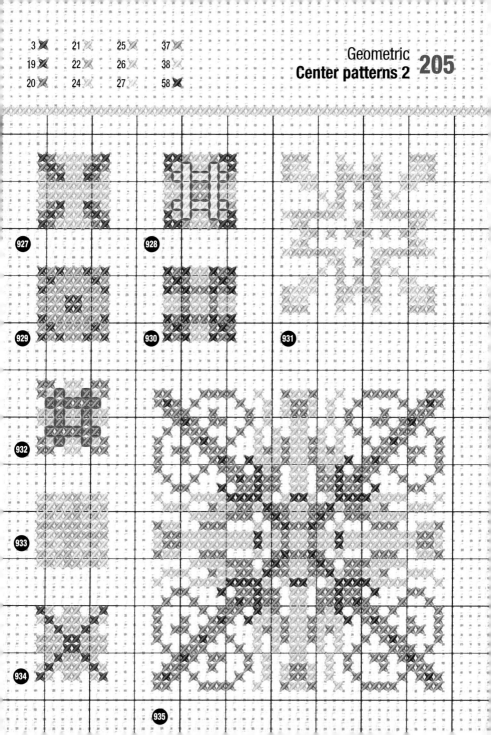

3 21 25 37
19 22 26 38
20 24 27 58

927

928

929

930

931

932

933

934

935

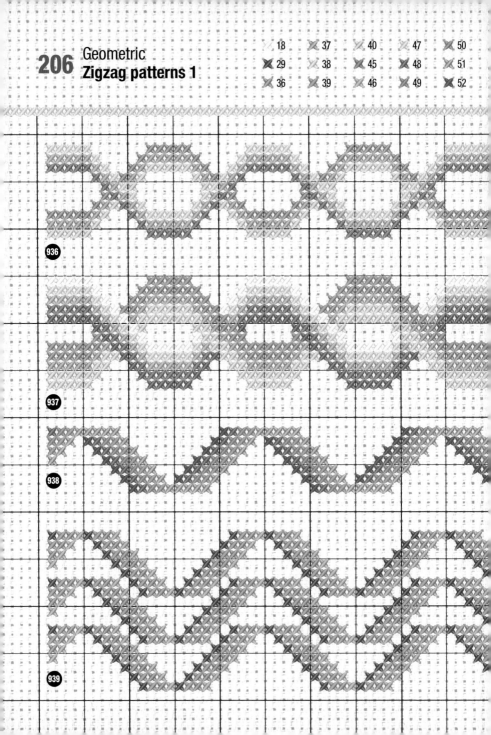

18   37   40   47   50
29   38   45   48   51
36   39   46   49   52

936

937

938

939

32 ╳   40 ╳   47 ╳   51 ╳
38 ╳   45 ╳   48 ╳   53 ╳
39 ╳   46 ╳   49 ╳   54 ╳

Geometric
Zigzag patterns 2 207

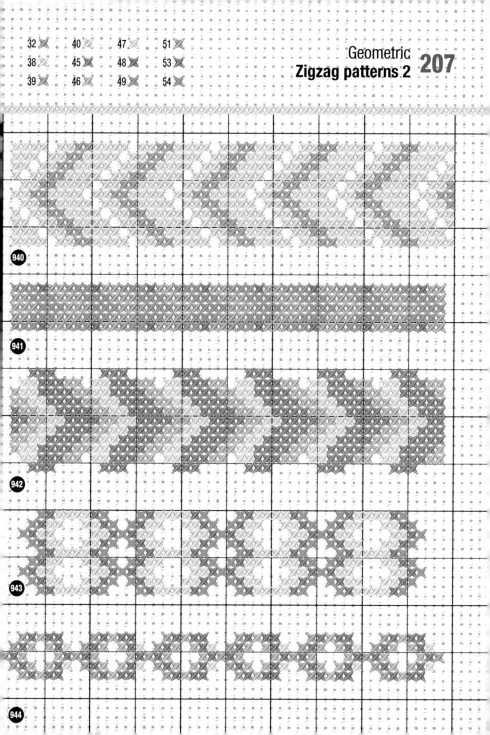

940

941

942

943

944

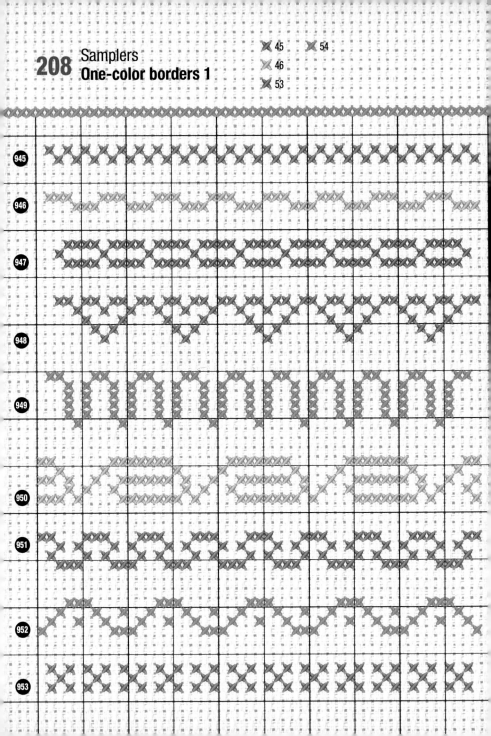

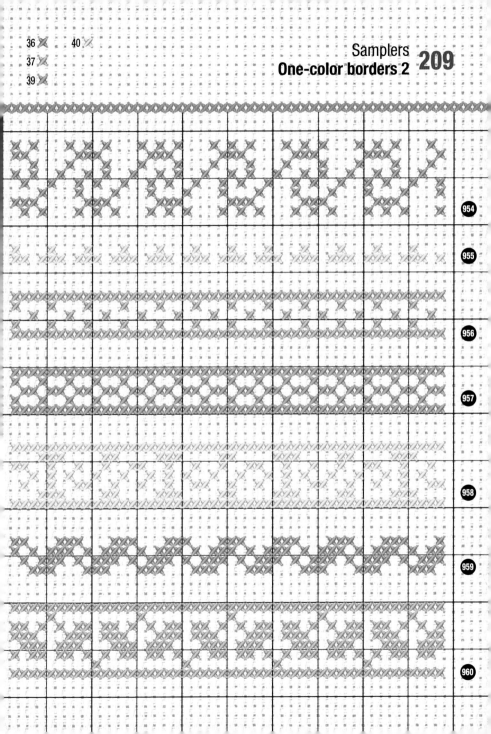

954

955

956

957

958

959

960

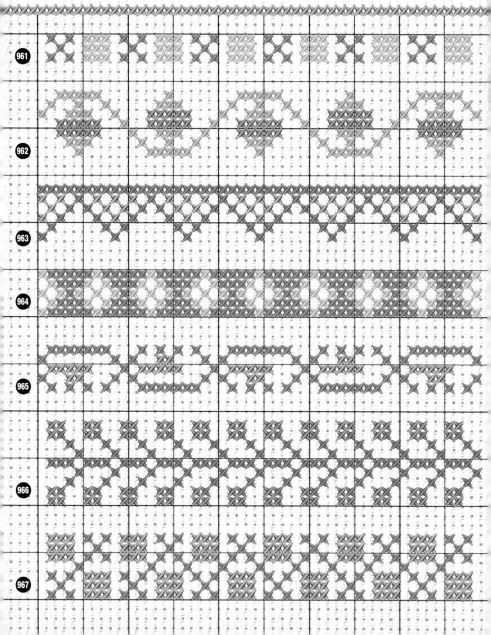

20 ✕   45 ✕
23 ✕   46 ✕
43 ✕   53 ✕

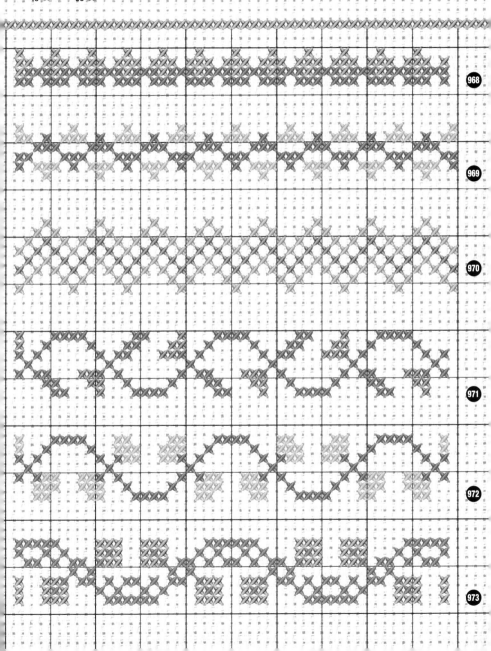

968
969
970
971
972
973

✖ 15   ✕ 18   ✖ 51
✕ 16   ✖ 45   ✖ 53
✕ 17   ✖ 50

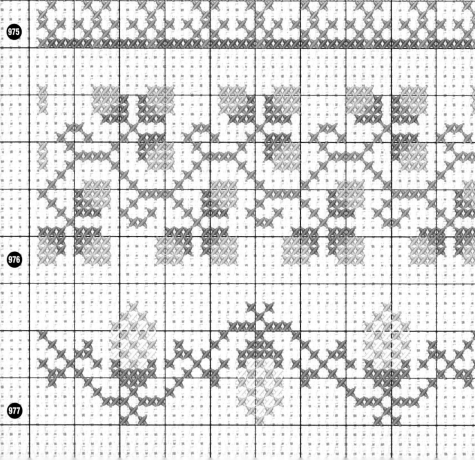

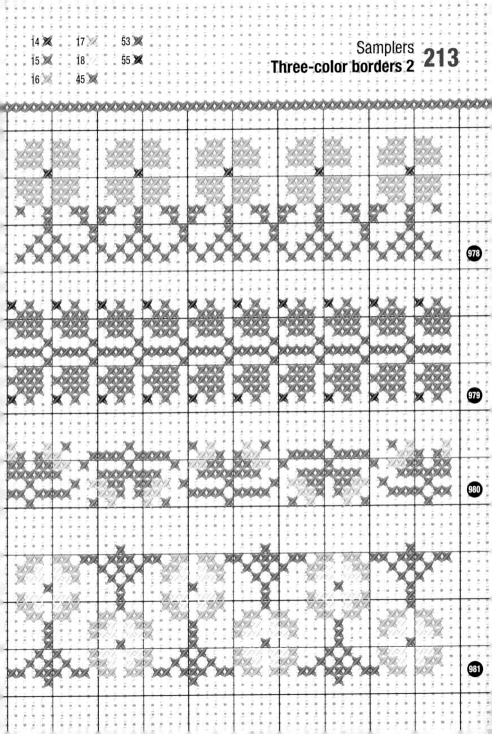

978

979

980

981

⊠ 17 ✖ 41 ⊠ 45 ✖ 52
⊠ 20 ✖ 42 ⊠ 46
⊠ 21 ✖ 43 ⊠ 47

982

983

984

14 ✕ 42 ✕ 46 ✕
21 ✕ 43 ✕ 47 ✕
41 ✕ 45 ✕ 52 ✕

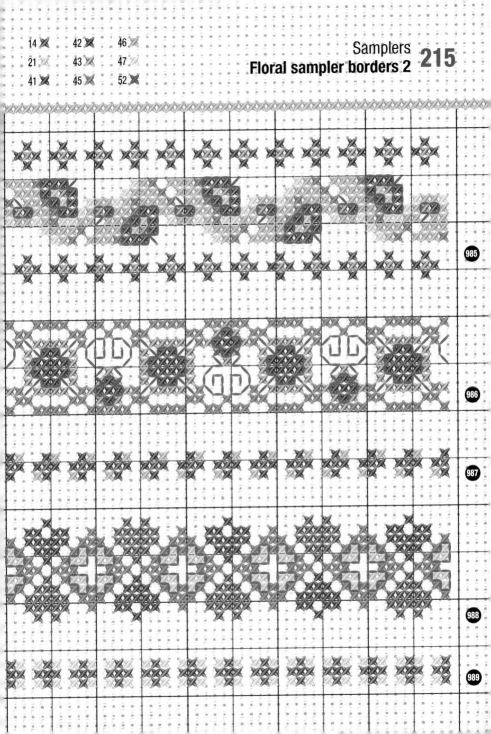

985

986

987

988

989

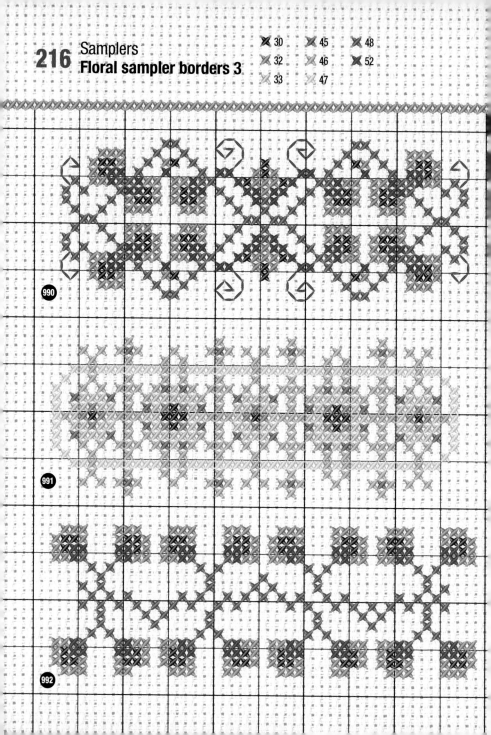

28 ✕ 42 ✕ 52 ✕
30 ✕ 43 ✕ 53 ✕
32 ✕ 45 ✕

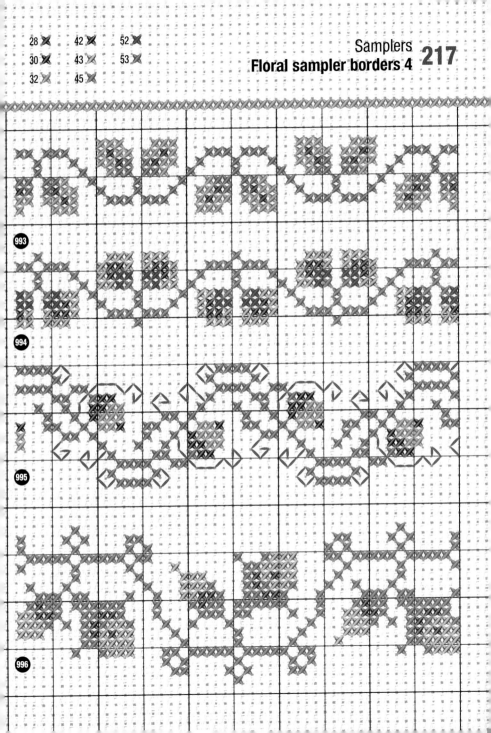

993

994

995

996

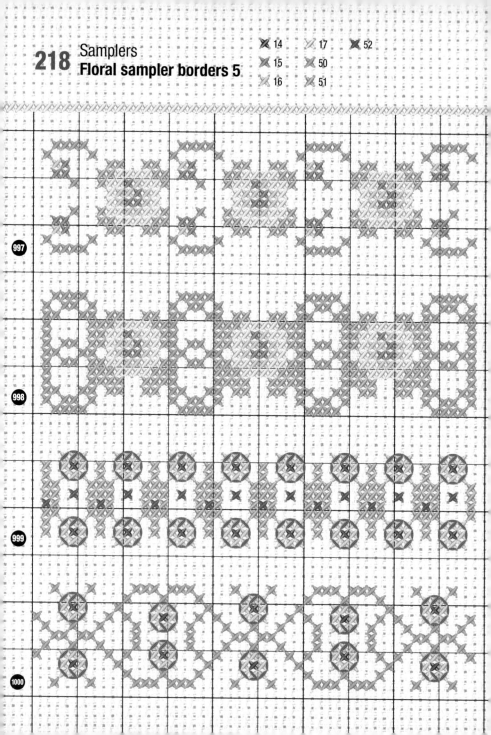

14 ✖ 17 ✖ 49 ✖ 55 ✖
15 ✖ 18   50 ✖
16 ✖ 45 ✖ 51 ✖

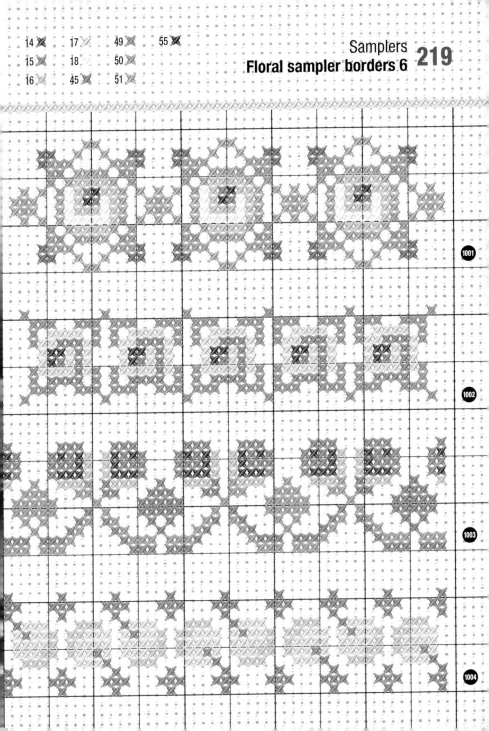

1001

1002

1003

1004

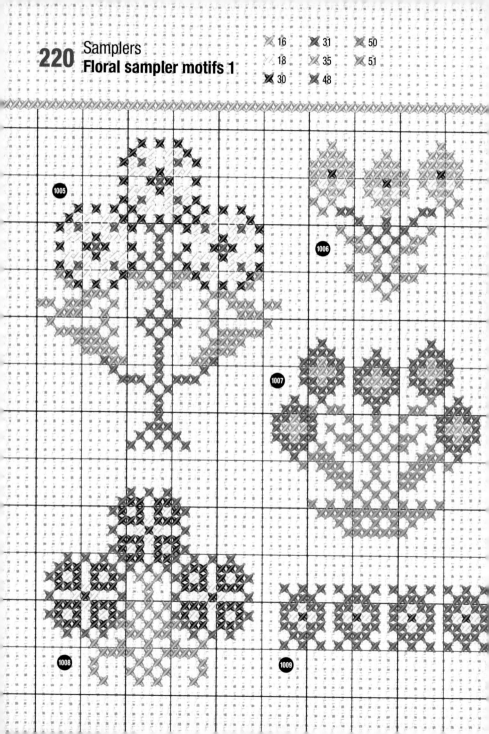

16 | 35 | 45 | 53
18 | 42 | 48
30 | 43 | 52

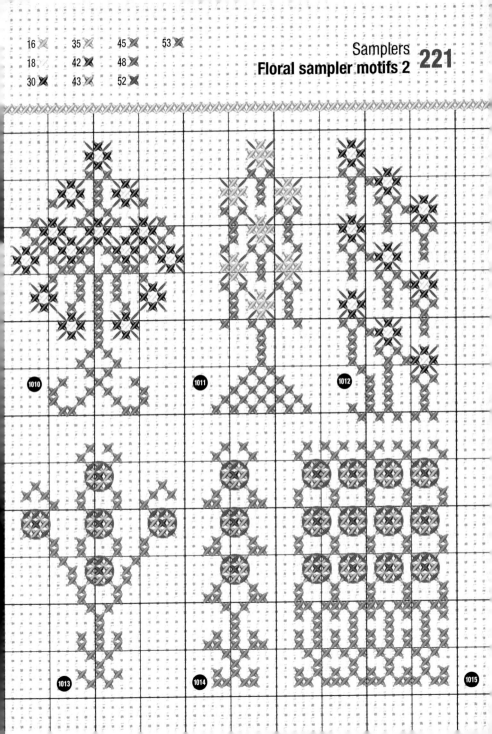

1010

1011

1012

1013

1014

1015

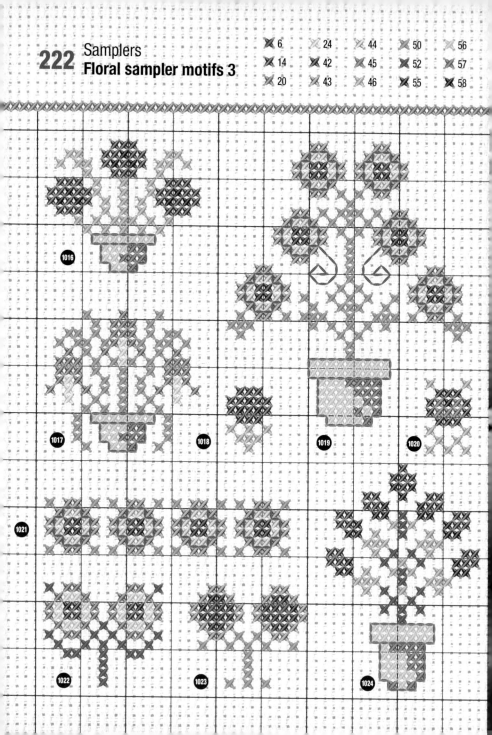

6 ✖	45 ✖	51 ✖	55 ✖
20 ✖	46 ✖	52 ✖	56 ✖
22 ✖	49 ✖	53 ✖	57 ✖

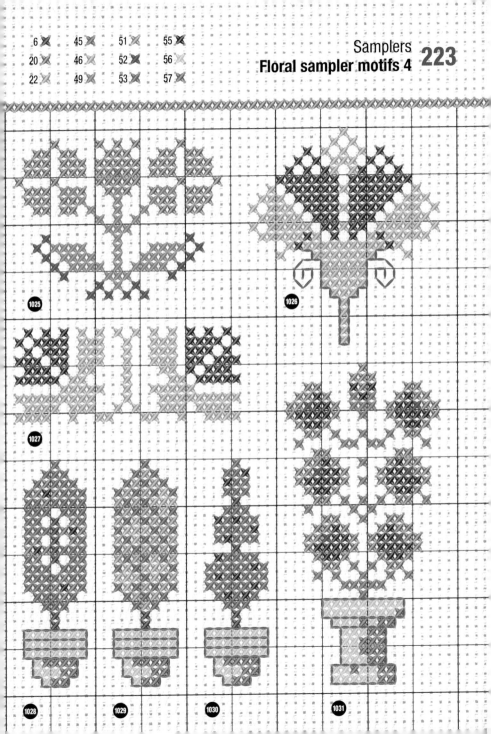

1025
1026
1027
1028
1029
1030
1031

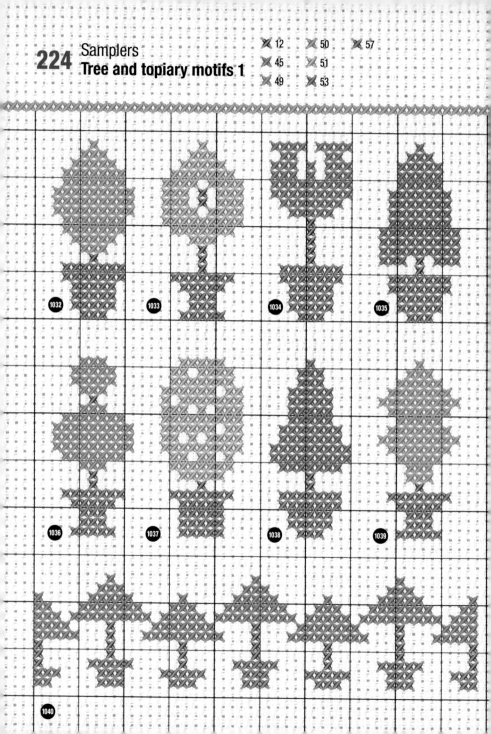

6 ✕   46 ✕   52 ✕   56 ✕
12 ✕   47 ✕   53 ✕   57 ✕
45 ✕   50 ✕   54 ✕

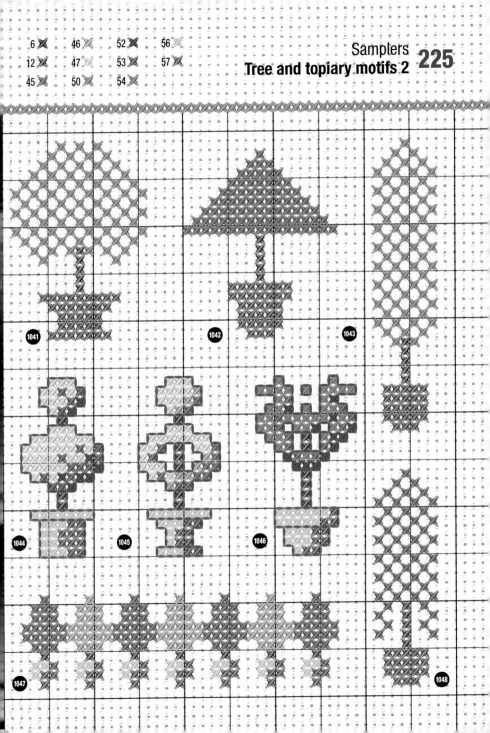

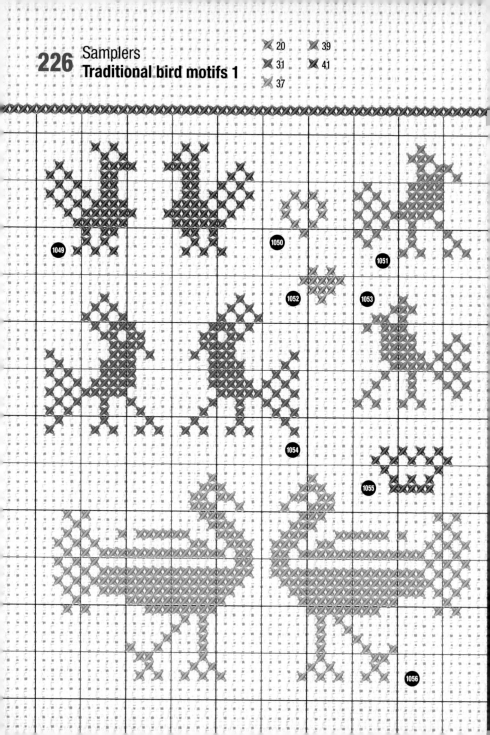

20 21 23 29 36 41

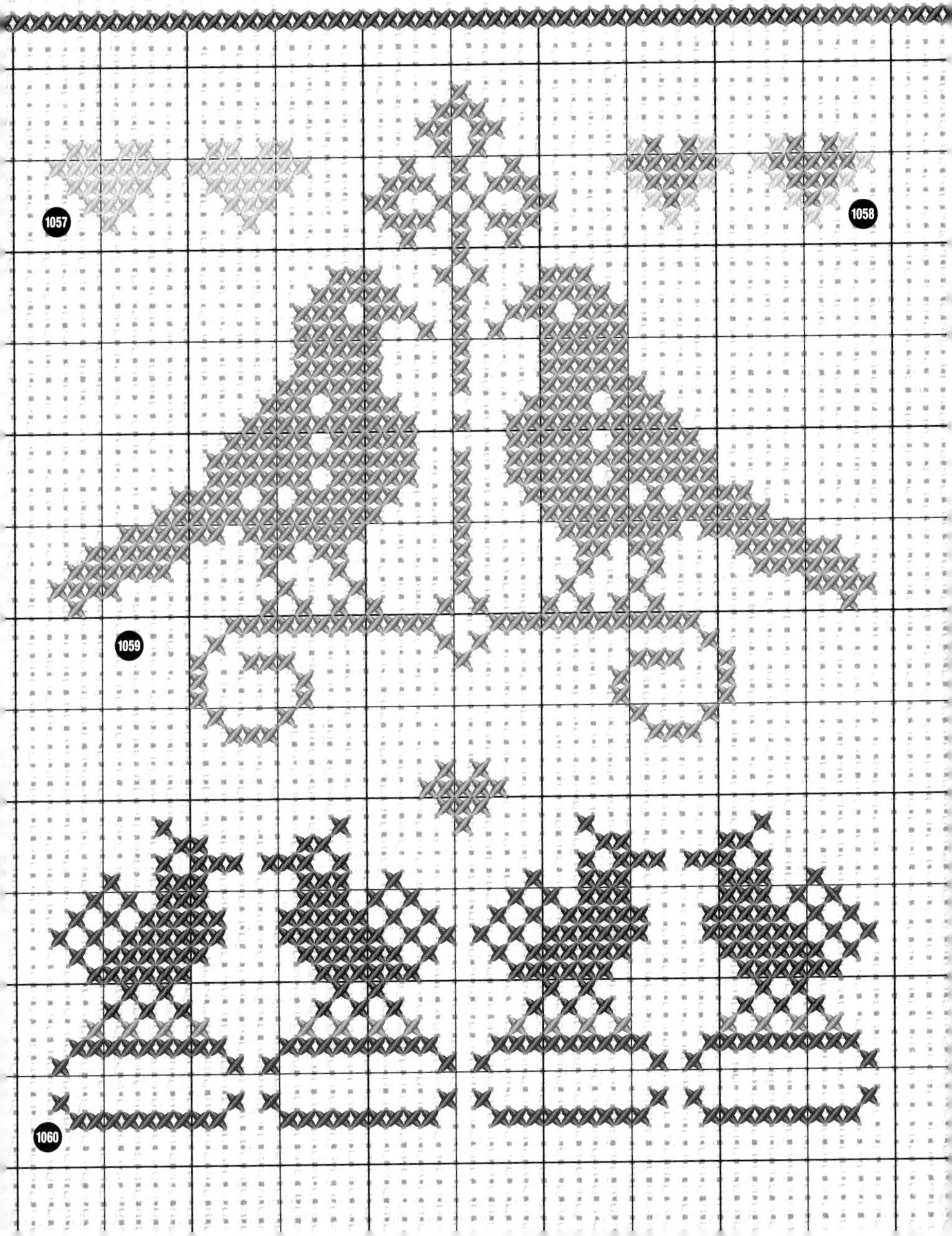

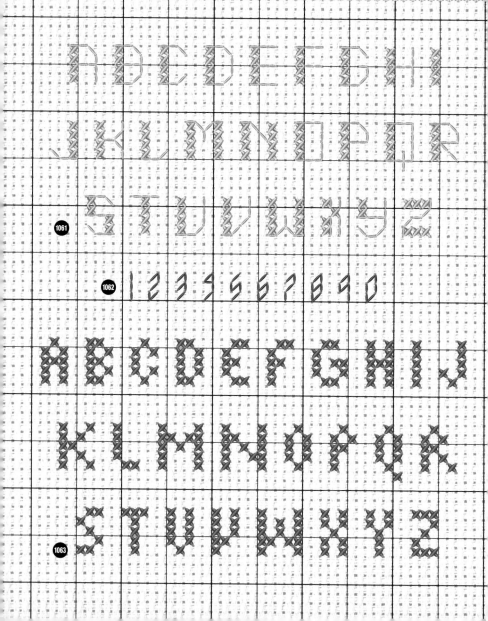

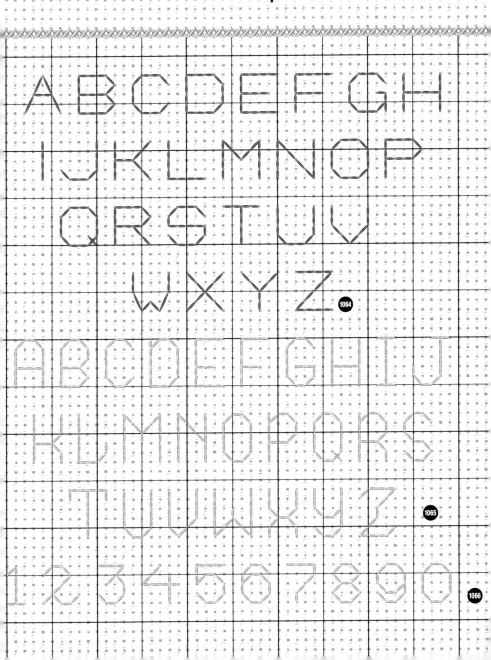

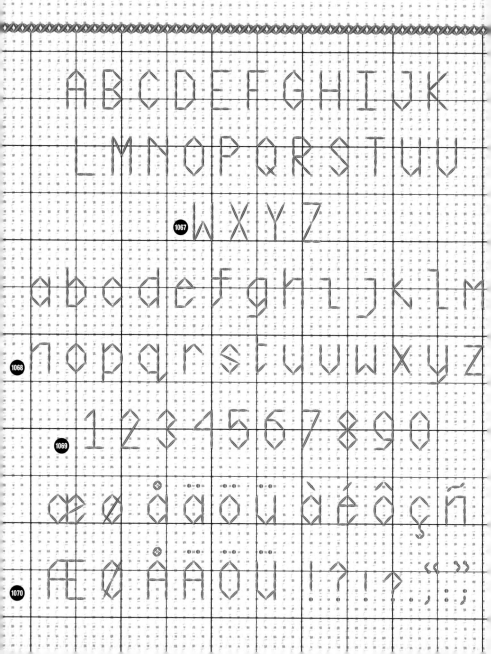

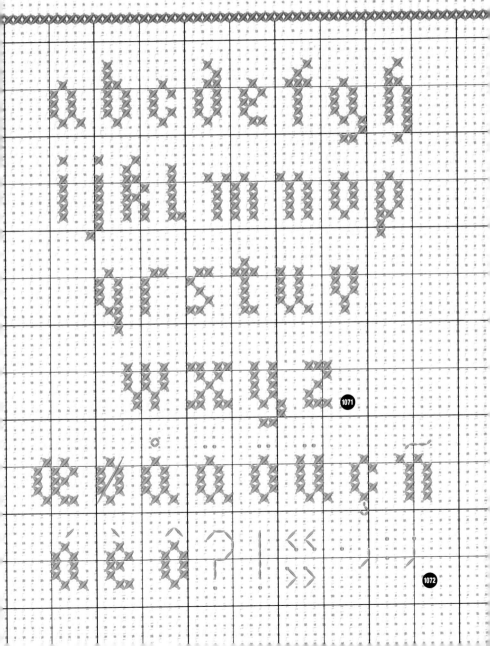

✖ 42
✖ 43
✖ 44

1073

A B C D
E F G H
I J K L M
N O P Q
R S T U

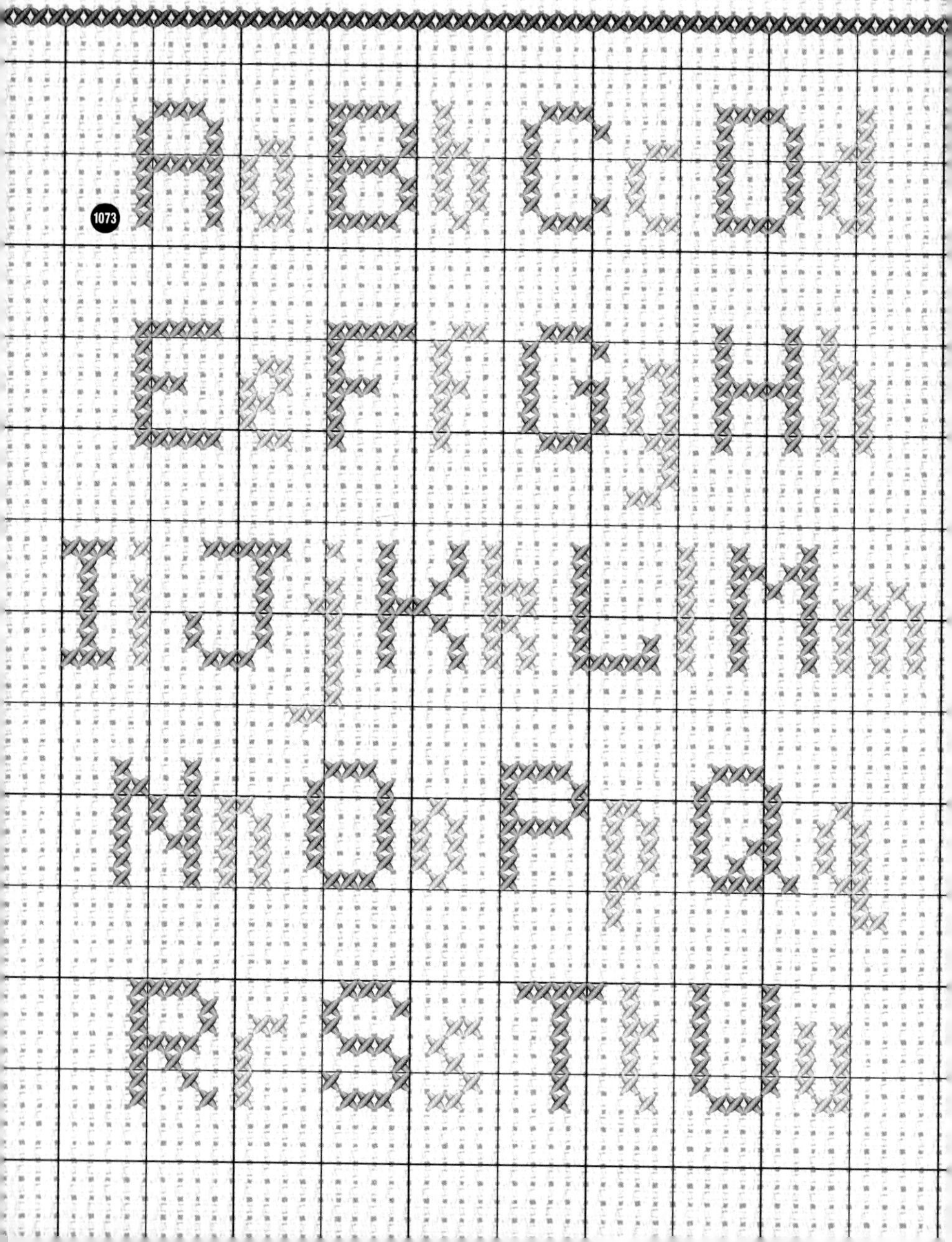

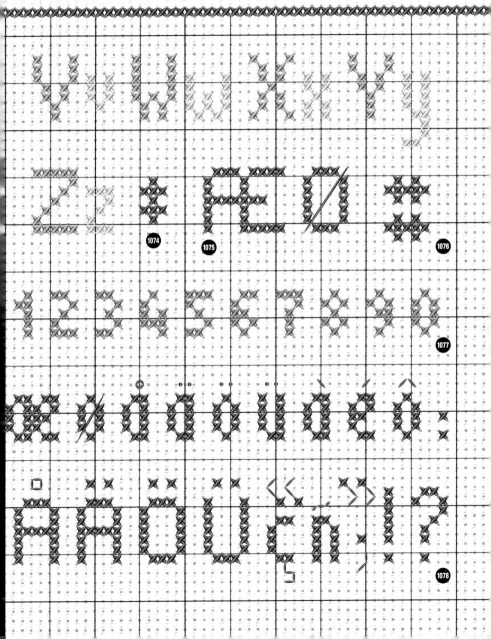

✖ 48
✖ 51

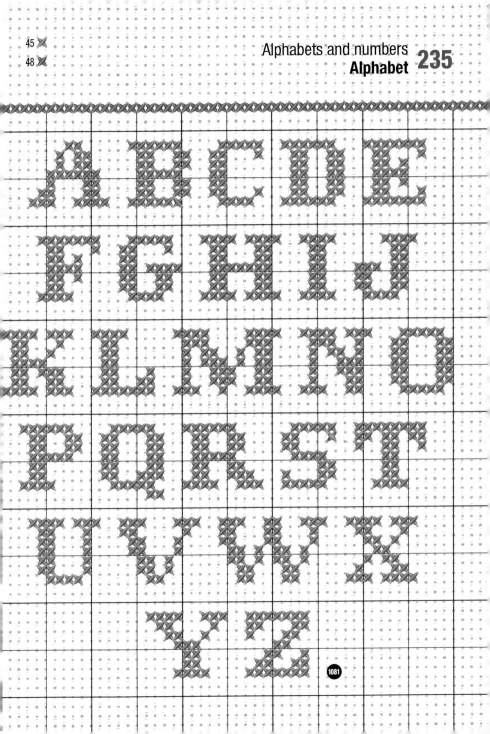

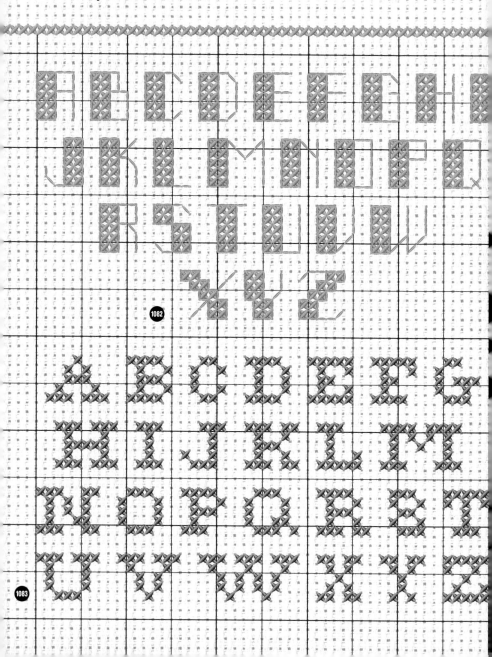

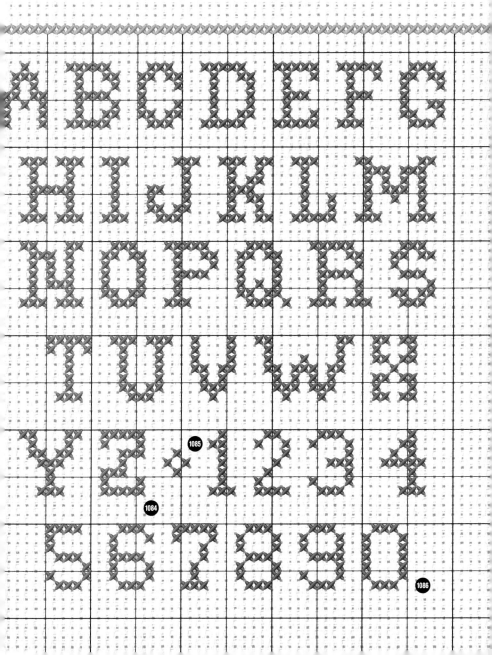

1087

19
20
21

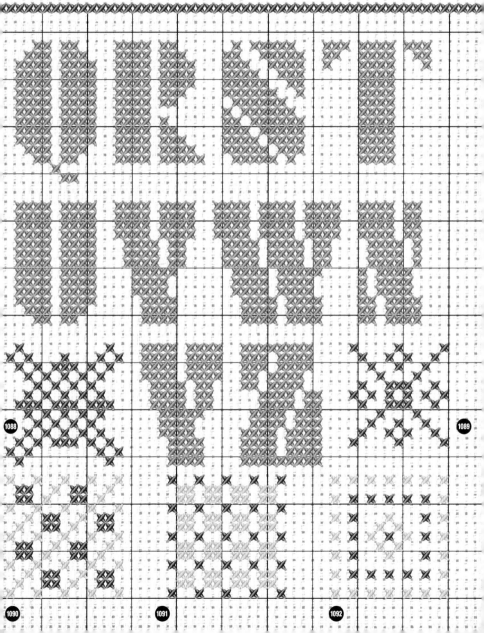

1088

1089

1090

1091

1092

✕ 31
✕ 40

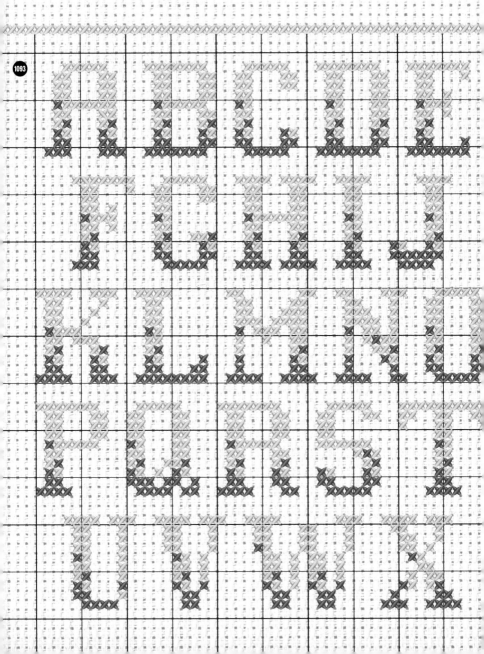

31 ✖ 40 ✖
32 ✖
38 ✖

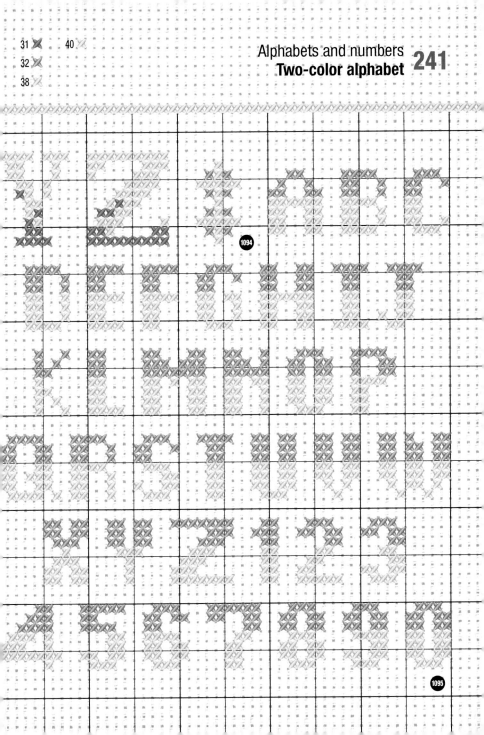

1094

1095

242 Alphabets and numbers
Condensed alphabet

✕ 50

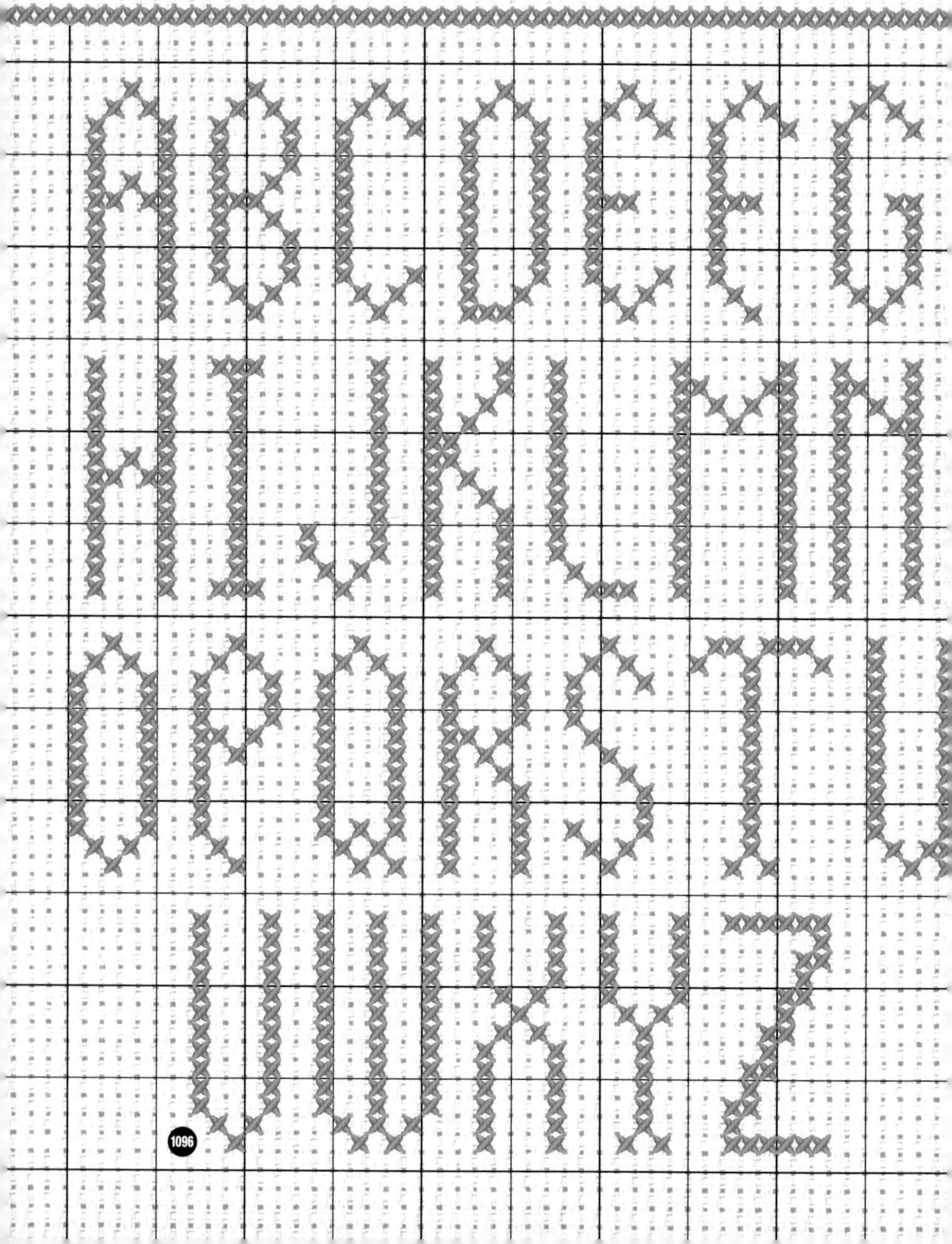

1096

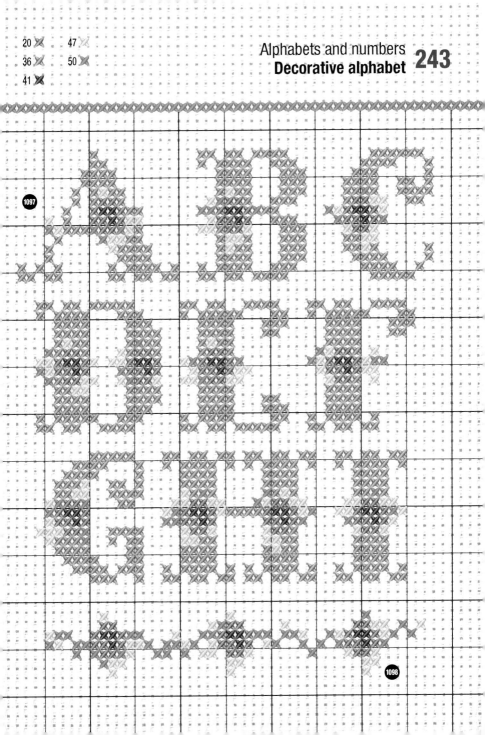

20 47
36 50
41

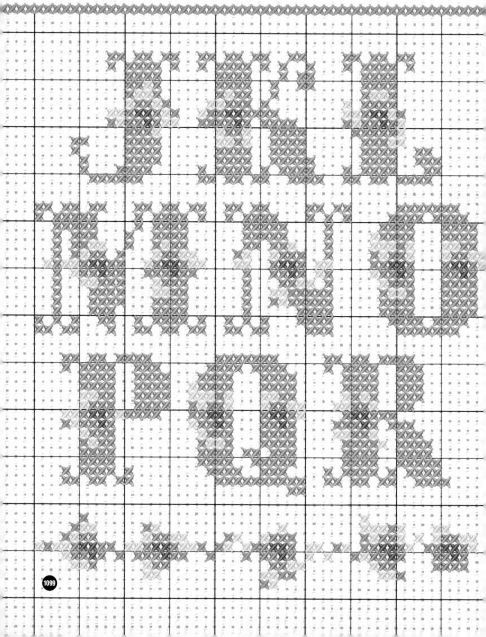

20   47
36 50
41

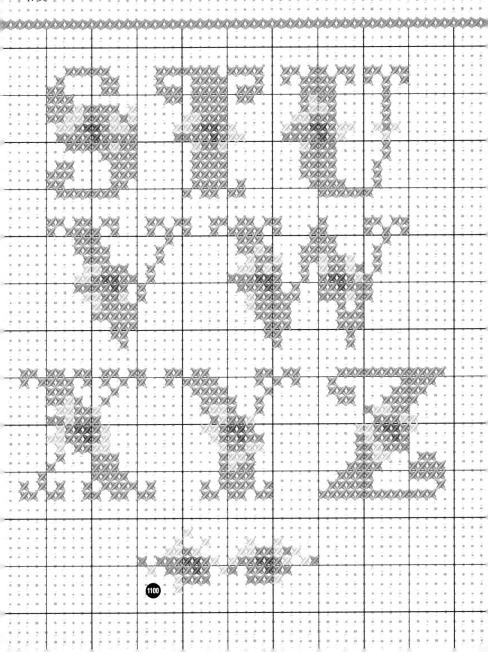

✕ 3   ✕ 28   ✕ 46
✕ 16   ✕ 29
✕ 17   ✕ 32

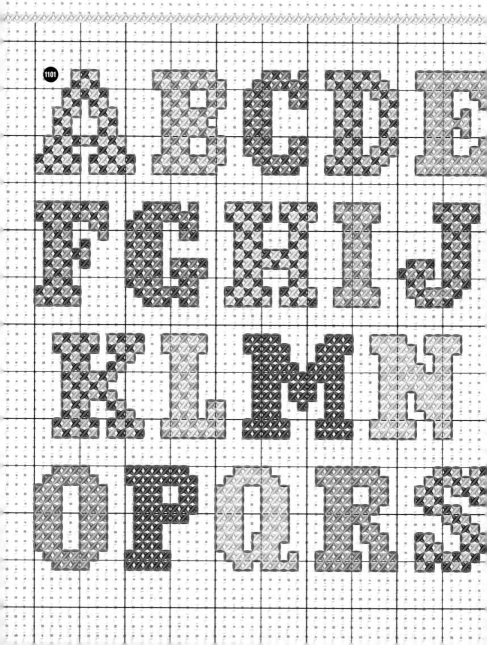

1101

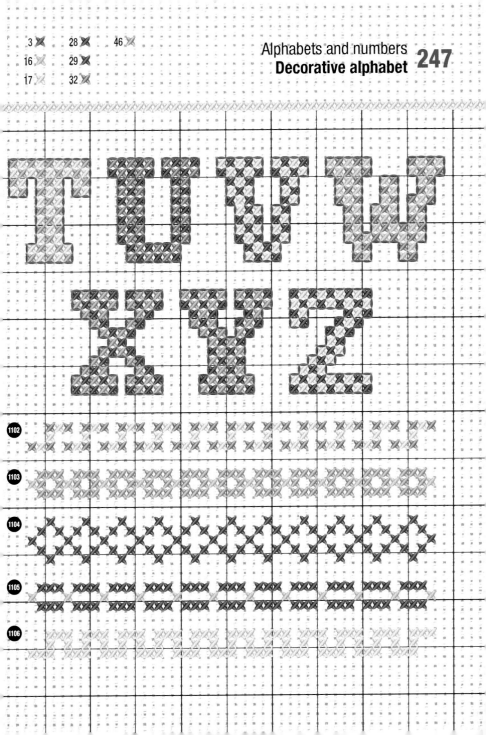

✖ 12
✖ 13
✖ 15

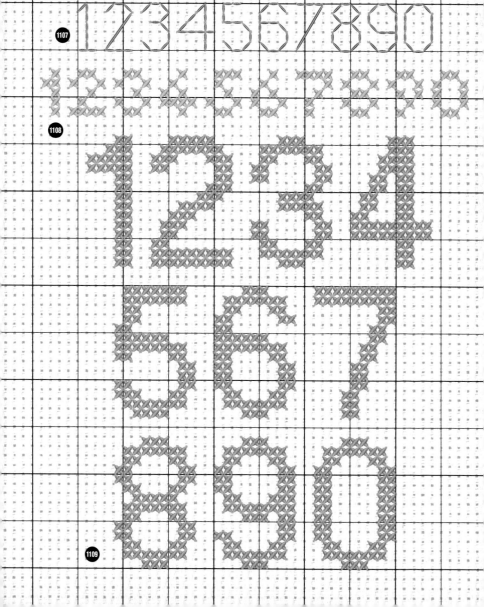

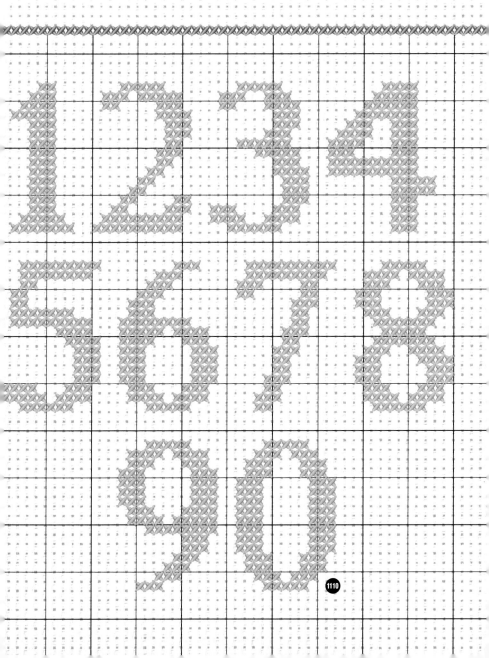

1110

250

List of sizes

Motif measurements are given as height x width, in numbers of stitches. Borders have either a height or width measurement, depending on the horizontal or vertical position of the border on the page. Alphabets and numbers have height measurements.

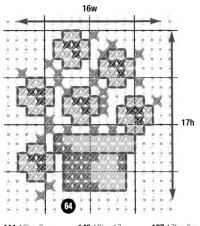

16w

17h

64

FLOWERS
1 42h x 8w
2 17h x 16w
3 16h x 17w
4 16h x 17w
5 17h x 16w
6 18h x 41w
7 18h x 12w
8 4h x 13w
9 4h x 18w
10 18h x 12w
11 14h x 8w
12 23h x 25w
13 13h x 6w
14 18h x 12w
15 4h x 18w
16 4h x 13w
17 18h x 12w
18 23h x 23w
19 18h x 17w
20 6w
21 12h
22 51h x 50w
23 28h
24 12h
25 11h
26 17h
27 12h x 11w
28 12h x 11w
29 12h x 11w
30 20h
31 20h
32 27h x 15w
33 33h x 33w
34 24h x 9w
35 15h
36 37h x 37w
37 37h x 8w

38 32h x 33w
39 19h x 8w
40 9h x 13w
41 5h
42 15h
43 23h x 22w
44 24h x 24w
45 18h x 17w
46 18h x 17w
47 18h x 17w
48 11w
49 49h x 29w
50 49h x 29w
51 6w
52 39h x 39w
53 13h x 13w
54 13h x 13w
55 13h x 13w
56 24h x 24w
57 24h x 24w
58 23h x 23w
59 12w
60 14h x 14w
61 14h x 14w
62 39h x 34w
63 50h x 22w
64 50h x 22w
65 18h x 16w
66 17h
67 17h
68 19h
69 4h
70 7h
71 8h
72 9h
73 7h
74 7h
75 13h

76 18h
77 18h
78 10h
79 20h
80 20h

HOME AND GARDEN
81 38h x 21w
82 38h x 21w
83 7h x 7w
84 17h x 26w
85 21h x 26w
86 21h x 26w
87 5h x 15w
88 4h x 6w
89 43h x 22w
90 23h x 25w
91 43h x 22w
92 12h x 48w
93 23h x 45w
94 33h x 43w
95 17h x 20w
96 15h x 24w
97 18h x 30w
98 18h x 11w
99 14h x 42w
100 44h x 19w
101 46h x 21w
102 16h x 6w
103 16h x 6w
104 16h x 6w
105 16h x 6w
106 16h x 6w
107 4h
108 12h
109 16h x 6w
110 16h x 6w

111 16h x 6w
112 16h x 6w
113 16h x 6w
114 16h x 6w
115 16h x 6w
116 16h x 6w
117 16h x 6w
118 16h x 6w
119 3h x 8w
120 3h x 8w
121 6h x 7w
122 6h x 7w
123 7h x 2w
124 2h x 7w
125 2h x 7w
126 7h x 2w
127 6h x 11w
128 6h x 11w
129 18h x 8w
130 18h x 8w
131 18h x 8w
132 18h x 8w
133 12h x 10w
134 12h x 10w
135 12h x 10w
136 12h x 10w
137 12h x 10w
138 12h x 10w
139 12h x 10w
140 12h x 10w
141 12h x 10w
142 12h x 10w
143 12h x 10w
144 12h x 10w
145 12h x 10w
146 12h x 10w
147 12h x 10w
148 12h x 10w

149 12h x 17w
150 12h x 17w
151 13h x 6w
152 20h x 11w
153 16h x 12w
154 26h x 22w
155 26h x 22w
156 15h x 15w
157 21h x 17w
158 17h x 11w
159 17h x 11w
160 36h x 20w
161 14h x 9w
162 14h x 9w
163 10w
164 5h x 5w
165 9h x 9w
166 8h x 8w
167 31h x 29w
168 4w
169 28h x 13w
170 28h x 13w
171 21h x 29w
172 17h x 10w
173 28h x 37w
174 16h x 18w
175 9w
176 41h x 41w
177 13h x 24w
178 13h x 24w
179 36h x 38w
180 33h x 15w
181 20h x 8w
182 19h x 15w
183 17h x 7w
184 17h x 7w
185 27h x 11w
186 17h x 6w

187 17h x 6w
188 27h x 9w
189 17h x 6w
190 17h x 6w
191 13h x 14w
192 5h
193 22h x 30w
194 4h x 4w
195 33h x 10w
196 46h x 44w
197 9h x 13w
198 9h x 13w
199 9h x 13w
200 46h x 44w
201 9h x 13w
202 9h x 13w
203 9h x 13w

NATURAL WORLD
204 36h x 35w
205 32h x 15w
206 20h x 20w
207 22h x 22w
208 26h x 25w
209 17h x 17w
210 13h x 13w
211 15h x 15w
212 32h x 32w
213 23h x 23w
214 16h x 12w
215 18h x 18w
216 25h x 23w
217 15h x 12w
218 7w
219 19h x 24w
220 10h x 15w
221 8h x 16w

222 10h x 12w	**273** 12h x 18w	**322** 18h x 5w	**373** 7h x 9w	**425** 4h	**474** 3h
223 14h x 9w	**274** 10h	**323** 37h x 9w	**374** 7h x 11w	**426** 17h	**475** 7h
224 3h x 5w	**275** 13h x 23w	**324** 37h x 9w	**375** 12h x 19w	**427** 8h	**476** 6h
225 5h x 3w	**276** 13h x 23w	**325** 20h x 16w	**376** 18h x 26w	**428** 15h x 40w	**477** 12h x 35w
226 12h x 10w	**277** 56h x 22w	**326** 15h x 11w	**377** 6h	**429** 29h x 25w	**478** 7h
227 7h x 7w	**278** 10h x 22w	**327** 15h x 11w	**378** 6h x 9w	**430** 15h x 13w	**479** 10h
228 7h x 7w	**279** 10h x 22w	**328** 7w	**379** 6h x 7w	**431** 15h x 13w	**480** 19h x 19w
229 7h x 7w	**280** 10h x 22w	**329** 4w	**380** 9h x 9w	**432** 19h	**481** 5h x 5w
230 7h x 7w	**281** 18h x 18w	**330** 19h x 11w	**381** 18h x 26w	**433** 19h x 22w	**482** 19h x 19w
231 8h x 16w	**282** 12h x 21w	**331** 19h x 11w	**382** 7h x 11w	**434** 19h x 22w	**483** 14h x 18w
232 23h x 23w	**283** 12h x 21w	**332** 4w	**383** 6h x 7w	**435** 26h x 25w	**484** 9w
233 23h x 23w	**284** 12h x 21w	**333** 18h x 15w	**384** 12h x 13w	**436** 24h x 17w	**485** 20h x 13w
234 6h	**285** 12h x 21w	**334** 17h x 13w	**385** 4h x 5w	**437** 8h	**486** 5w
235 23h x 23w	**286** 12h x 21w	**335** 17h x 17w	**386** 7h x 9w	**438** 19h x 12w	**487** 16h x 21w
236 23h x 23w	**287** 12h x 21w	**336** 17h x 17w	**387** 10h x 11w	**439** 24h	**488** 19h x 19w
237 13h x 13w	**288** 12h x 21w	**337** 34h x 34w	**388** 5h x 5w	**440** 15h x 19w	**489** 57h x 45w
238 13h x 13w	**289** 12h x 21w	**338** 12h x 10w	**389** 12h x 13w	**441** 6h x 10w	**490** 9h x 17w
239 22h x 25w	**290** 9h x 19w	**339** 9h x 10w	**390** 3h x 3w	**442** 12h x 11w	**491** 14h x 11w
240 9h x 9w	**291** 20h x 27w	**340** 9h x 10w	**391** 19h x 24w	**443** 7h	**492** 5h x 5w
241 9h x 9w	**292** 16h x 18w	**341** 30h x 13w	**392** 7h x 7w	**444** 24h x 48w	**493** 5h x 12w
242 8h x 8w	**293** 8h x 10w	**342** 11h x 12w	**393** 12h x 11w	**445** 31h x 49w	**494** 14h x 9w
243 14h x 15w	**294** 12h x 25w	**343** 11h x 12w	**394** 7h x 23w	**446** 9h x 48w	**495** 9h
244 12h x 12w	**295** 20h x 27w	**344** 18h x 15w	**395** 16h x 21w	**447** 46h x 46w	**496** 43h x 43w
245 12h x 14w	**296** 14h x 18w	**345** 15h x 12w	**396** 12h x 23w		**497** 3w
246 12h x 12w	**297** 10h	**346** 18h x 15w	**397** 4h	**CULTURAL**	**498** 21h x 21w
247 24h x 27w	**298** 10h	**347** 18h x 15w	**398** 10h x 11w	**448** 12h	**499** 21h x 21w
248 15h x 13w	**299** 11h	**348** 8h x 9w	**399** 25h x 29w	**449** 7h	**500** 5w
249 24h x 37w	**300** 11h	**349** 18h x 15w	**400** 10h x 11w	**450** 12h	**501** 35h x 35w
250 14h x 17w	**301** 19h	**350** 21h x 15w	**401** 4h	**451** 15h	**502** 27h
251 14h x 17w	**302** 19h x 28w	**351** 38h x 31w	**402** 3h	**452** 7h	**503** 28h
252 24h x 32w	**303** 14h x 22w	**352** 23h x 15w	**403** 6h	**453** 12h	**504** 45h x 45w
253 14h x 17w	**304** 14h x 22w	**353** 7h	**404** 22h x 26w	**454** 12h	**505** 11h x 11w
254 14h x 17w	**305** 25h x 10w	**354** 16h	**405** 3w	**455** 14h	**506** 11h x 11w
255 25h x 32w	**306** 53h x 43w	**355** 23h x 12w	**406** 14w	**456** 27h x 36w	**507** 11h x 11w
256 34h x 16w	**307** 17h x 11w	**356** 17h x 11w	**407** 5w	**457** 27h x 36w	**508** 11h x 11w
257 30h x 26w	**308** 7w	**357** 10h x 13w	**408** 9h x 10w	**458** 6w	**509** 45h x 45w
258 42h x 25w	**309** 54h x 24w	**358** 30h x 23w	**409** 5w	**459** 12h x 7w	**510** 11h x 11w
259 35h x 23w	**310** 10h x 18w	**359** 14h x 7w	**410** 15h x 15w	**460** 12h x 7w	**511** 11h x 11w
260 14h	**311** 10h x 14w	**360** 9h	**411** 12h	**461** 12h x 7w	**512** 11h x 11w
261 5h	**312** 10h x 17w	**361** 8h	**412** 6h	**462** 12h x 7w	**513** 11h x 11w
262 32h x 48w	**313** 10h x 14w	**362** 8h	**413** 58h x 14w	**463** 25h x 15w	**514** 30h x 31w
263 18h	**314** 10h x 14w	**363** 5h	**414** 19h x 8w	**464** 32h x 9w	**515** 24h x 12w
264 24h x 15w		**364** 8h	**415** 16h x 13w	**465** 25h x 14w	**516** 23h x 45w
265 18h x 21w	**CELEBRATIONS**	**365** 7h	**416** 35h x 25w	**466** 24h x 14w	**517** 12w
266 15h x 13w	**315** 19h x 13w	**366** 4h	**417** 20h	**467** 25h x 14w	**518** 18h x 29w
267 18h x 3w	**316** 19h x 13w	**367** 7h	**418** 14h	**468** 7h	**519** 31h x 31w
268 20h x 13w	**317** 19h x 15w	**368** 12h	**419** 9h	**469** 21h	**520** 27h x 19w
269 5w	**318** 14h x 10w	**369** 3h	**420** 8h x 7w	**470** 7h	**521** 49h x 40w
270 10h	**319** 14h x 10w	**370** 23h	**421** 8h x 7w	**471** 15h	**522** 14h
271 12h x 18w	**320** 18h x 5w	**371** 8h	**423** 15h x 13w	**472** 9h	**523** 27h x 19w
272 12h x 8w	**321** 18h x 5w	**372** 15h x 21w	**424** 26h x 18w	**473** 19h	**524** 27h x 19w

252 List of sizes

525 25h	**574** 28h x 23w	**625** 11h x 34w
526 21h x 32w	**575** 8w	**626** 3h
527 13h	**576** 29h x 37w	**627** 15h x 31w
528 13h	**577** 8h	**628** 7h x 11w
529 13h	**578** 16h	**629** 10h x 10w
530 12h	**579** 15w	**630** 12w
531 12h	**580** 16h x 25w	**631** 5h x 5w
532 13h	**581** 38h x 27w	**632** 5h x 5w
533 13h	**582** 21h	**633** 10h x 10w
534 11h	**583** 21h	**634** 29h x 29w
	584 9h	
HISTORY	**585** 4h	**HOBBIES AND**
535 56h x 31w	**586** 7h	**OCCUPATIONS**
536 16h x 13w	**587** 20h x 20w	**635** 34h x 16w
537 30h x 8w	**588** 19h x 19w	**636** 33h x 15w
538 31h x 25w	**589** 8h	**637** 33h x 14w
539 13h	**590** 4h	**638** 33h x 13w
540 11h	**591** 9h	**639** 33h x 12w
541 9h x 6w	**592** 7h	**640** 43h x 12w
542 26h x 17w	**593** 5h	**641** 33h x 16w
543 12h x 10w	**594** 8h	**642** 33h x 13w
544 26h x 17w	**595** 12h	**643** 33h x 14w
545 31h x 23w	**596** 16h x 16w	**644** 34h x 17w
546 31h x 23w	**597** 16h x 16w	**645** 33h x 14w
547 4h x 9w	**598** 16h x 16w	**646** 33h x 14w
548 21h x 14w	**599** 16h x 16w	**647** 17h x 17w
549 4h x 9w	**600** 16h x 16w	**648** 17h x 17w
550 22h	**601** 16h x 16w	**649** 17h x 17w
551 8w	**602** 8w	**650** 17h x 17w
552 22h x 34w	**603** 17h x 17w	**651** 37h x 46w
553 10h	**604** 17h x 17w	**652** 14h
554 22h x 34w	**605** 17h x 17w	**653** 12h x 14w
555 21h x 21w	**606** 17h x 17w	**654** 5h x 10w
556 26h x 24w	**607** 5w	**655** 6h x 7w
557 26h x 26w	**608** 3h	**656** 7h x 8w
558 23h x 26w	**609** 12h	**657** 6h x 7w
559 26h x 24w	**610** 30h x 33w	**658** 25h x 20w
560 26h x 26w	**611** 19h x 8w	**659** 27h x 31w
561 9h x 49w	**612** 19h x 8w	**660** 8h x 8w
562 43h x 43w	**613** 23h x 23w	**661** 10h x 12w
563 44h x 44w	**614** 8w	**662** 4w
564 7h	**615** 5w	**663** 4w
565 17h x 17w	**616** 5w	**664** 17h x 11w
566 17h x 17w	**617** 17h x 19w	**665** 17h x 13w
567 21h x 50w	**618** 17h x 19w	**666** 17h x 13w
568 11h x 47w	**619** 24h x 24w	**667** 17h x 11w
569 56h x 44w	**620** 5w	**668** 4h
570 28h x 10w	**621** 9h x 7w	**669** 22h x 21w
571 28h x 10w	**622** 30h x 33w	**670** 22h x 21w
572 25h	**623** 42h x 46w	**671** 22h x 21w
573 26h x 21w	**624** 10h x 15w	**672** 22h x 21w

673 33h x 14w	**724** 16h x 12w	**773** 28h x 43w
674 33h x 12w	**725** 17h x 22w	**774** 26h x 17w
675 33h x 14w	**726** 16h x 16w	**775** 26h x 17w
676 35h x 14w	**727** 17h x 17w	**776** 26h x 17w
677 33h x 17w	**728** 12h x 17w	**777** 26h x 17w
678 33h x 16w	**729** 16h x 17w	**778** 26h x 3w
679 33h x 16w	**730** 15h x 15w	**779** 26h x 3w
680 33h x 15w	**731** 16h x 14w	**780** 26h x 3w
681 37h x 16w	**732** 8h x 19w	**781** 26h x 3w
682 33h x 15w	**733** 16h x 11w	**782** 26h x 3w
683 33h x 20w		**783** 26h x 3w
684 33h x 15w	**CHILDREN**	**784** 26h x 3w
685 11h x 20w	**734** 29h x 9w	**785** 26h x 3w
686 4h x 4w	**735** 26h x 32w	**786** 31h x 24w
687 7h	**736** 24h x 17w	**787** 4h x 24w
688 19h x 19w	**737** 24h x 29w	**788** 7h x 48w
689 4h x 4w	**738** 25h x 45w	**789** 11h x 31w
690 7h	**739** 20h x 43w	**790** 7h x 7w
691 8h x 18w	**740** 12h x 12w	**791** 1h x 7w
692 15h x 21w	**741** 12h x 12w	**793** 7h x 7w
693 5h x 31w	**742** 12h x 12w	**794** 31h x 24w
694 12h x 10w	**743** 12h x 12w	**795** 34h x 5w
695 21h x 8w	**744** 59h x 32w	**796** 8h x 8w
696 22h x 8w	**745** 24h x 21w	**797** 24h x 28w
697 21h x 8w	**746** 21h x 23w	**798** 24h x 19w
698 31h x 3w	**747** 31h x 31w	**799** 24h x 19w
699 31h x 5w	**748** 12w	**800** 32h x 26w
700 31h x 9w	**749** 11h	**801** 24h x 47w
701 31h x 3w	**750** 9h	**802** 11h
702 31h x 5w	**751** 3h	**803** 16h
703 31h x 3w	**752** 7h	**804** 42h x 38w
704 21h x 5w	**753** 12h	**805** 12h x 14w
705 21h x 5w	**754** 12h	**806** 12h x 14w
706 46h x 12w	**755** 15h	**807** 12h x 14w
707 31h x 8w	**756** 23h	**808** 35h x 27w
708 31h x 8w	**757** 33h x 32w	**809** 17h x 13w
709 14h x 11w	**758** 14h x 8w	**810** 12h x 13w
710 14h x 2w	**759** 14h x 8w	**811** 25h x 19w
711 8h x 20w	**760** 15h x 8w	**812** 40h x 42w
712 3h x 18w	**761** 15h x 8w	**813** 13h
713 14h x 11w	**762** 15h x 8w	**814** 40h x 42w
714 8h x 6w	**763** 15h x 8w	**815** 3h
715 8h x 6w	**764** 17h x 7w	**816** 9h
716 8h x 6w	**765** 17h x 7w	
717 8h x 6w	**766** 17h x 17w	**GEOMETRIC**
718 56h x 20w	**767** 20h	**817** 3h
719 25h x 24w	**768** 23h x 15w	**818** 5h
720 20h x 10w	**769** 16h	**819** 5h
721 24h x 14w	**770** 13h x 13w	**820** 5h
722 16h x 17w	**771** 14h x 30w	**821** 3h
723 16h x 17w	**772** 14h x 30w	**822** 5h

823 3h	874 33h x 24w	925 25h x 25w	977 13h	1028 24h x 7w	1076 7h x 5w
824 9h	875 21h x 21w	926 18h x 18w	978 13h	1029 24h x 7w	1077 5h
825 4h	876 20h x 20w	927 8h x 8w	979 11h	1030 24h x 7w	1078 9h
826 6h	877 20h x 20w	928 8h x 8w	980 7h	1031 34h x 17w	1079 7h
827 9h	878 11h x 24w	929 8h x 8w	981 15h	1032 19h x 9w	1080 7h
828 8h	879 21h x 21w	930 8h x 8w	982 12h	1033 19h x 9w	1081 7h
829 8h	880 15h x 23w	931 17h x 17w	983 11h	1034 19h x 9w	1082 5h
830 8h	881 13h x 20w	932 8h x 8w	984 27h	1035 19h x 9w	1083 5h
831 3h	882 33h x 25w	933 8h x 8w	985 15h	1036 19h x 9w	1084 7h
832 5h	883 20h x 20w	934 8h x 8w	986 10h	1037 19h x 9w	1085 3h x 3w
833 5h	884 10h x 10w	935 32h x 32w	987 3h	1038 19h x 9w	1086 7h
834 5h	885 10h x 10w	936 10h	988 11h	1039 19h x 9w	1087 13h
835 5h	886 10h x 10w	937 12h	989 3h	1040 12h	1088 13h x 13w
836 5h	887 10h x 10w	938 7h	990 17h	1041 21h x 15w	1089 11h x 11w
837 5h	888 8h x 8w	939 17h	991 17h	1042 20h x 17w	1090 13h x 13w
838 5h	889 8h x 8w	940 11h	992 16h	1043 31h x 7w	1091 13h x 13w
839 3h	890 8h x 8w	941 5h	993 8h	1044 19h x 9w	1092 13h x 13w
840 4h	891 8h x 8w	942 11h	994 8h	1045 19h x 9w	1093 10h
841 4h	892 19h x 19w	943 9h	995 13h	1046 19h x 11w	1094 9h x 5w
842 4h	893 19h x 19w	944 5h	996 17h	1047 10h	1095 7h
843 4h	894 19h x 19w		997 12h	1048 23h x 7w	1096 13h
844 6h	895 19h x 19w	**SAMPLERS**	998 13h	1049 12h x 23w	1097 14h
845 5h	896 19h x 19w	945 2h	999 10h	1050 5h x 5w	1098 7h x 42w
846 4h	897 19h x 19w	946 2h	1000 11h	1051 12h x 13w	1099 8h x 49w
847 2h	898 19h x 19w	947 3h	1001 14h	1052 4h x 5w	1100 7h x 20w
848 10h	899 19h x 19w	948 5h	1002 10h	1053 12h x 13w	1101 11h
849 8h	900 19h x 19w	949 6h	1003 12h	1054 15h x 28w	1102 3h
850 8h	901 8h	950 5h	1004 11h	1055 5h x 9w	1103 3h
851 11h	902 8h	951 4h	1005 33h x 27w	1056 22h x 46w	1104 5h
852 10h	903 12h	952 4h	1006 17h x 17w	1057 5h x 15w	1105 3h
853 13h	904 22h	953 3h	1007 21h x 23w	1058 5h x 15w	1106 3h
854 13h	905 26h x 26w	954 8h	1008 21h x 23w	1059 36h x 47w	1107 5h
855 13h	906 14h x 14w	955 2h	1009 7h x 23w	1060 20h x 47w	1108 5h
856 8h	907 14h x 14w	956 5h	1010 29h x 19w		1109 14h
857 25h x 25w	908 7h x 7w	957 5h	1011 29h x 11w	**ALPHABETS**	1110 16h
858 15h x 21w	909 17h x 20w	958 7h	1012 30h x 11w	**AND NUMBERS**	
859 15h x 21w	910 8h x 8w	959 4h	1013 26h x 17w	1061 4h	
860 30h x 25w	911 8h x 8w	960 8h	1014 26h x 7w	1062 3h	
861 41h x 21w	912 9h x 49w	961 3h	1015 26h x 17w	1063 5h	
862 32h x 48w	913 5h x 19w	962 7h	1016 14h x 17w	1064 4h	
863 25h x 49w	914 25h x 25w	963 6h	1017 15h x 17w	1065 5h	
864 15h x 21w	915 15h x 15w	964 5h	1018 7h x 5w	1066 4h	
865 15h x 21w	916 13h x 19w	968 4h	1019 30h x 27w	1067 4h	
866 21h x 21w	917 22h x 22w	969 6h	1020 8h x 5w	1068 5h	
867 36h x 21w	918 22h x 22w	970 8h	1021 6h x 27w	1069 4h	
868 20h x 23w	919 7h	971 7h	1022 11h x 13w	1070 5h	
869 28h x 21w	920 47h x 47w	972 7h	1023 11h x 13w	1071 9h	
870 15h x 25w	921 28h x 28w	973 7h	1024 24h x 17w	1072 8h	
871 10h x 25w	922 11h x 11w	974 10h	1025 17h x 23w	1073 10h	
872 28h x 28w	923 5h x 5w	975 6h	1026 23h x 21w	1074 5h x 3w	
873 28h x 14w	924 17h x 17w	976 19h	1027 10h x 25w	1075 7h	

THREAD CONVERSION CHART

Key number and name	DMC floss	Anchor floss	Key number and name	DMC floss	Anchor floss
1 white	blanc	2	30 royal blue	797	132
2 black	310	403	31 dark Delft blue	798	146
3 very dark pewter gray	3799	236	32 Delft blue	809	130
4 dark steel gray	414	235	33 very light violet-blue	3747	120
5 pearl gray	415	398	34 dark electric blue	995	410
6 very dark mocha brown	3031	905	35 medium electric blue	996	433
7 medium beige-brown	840	1084	36 light Wedgwood	518	1039
8 medium light antique gold	832	907	37 medium light peacock blue	376	167
9 medium light beige-gray	644	830	38 very light sky blue	747	158
10 ecru	ecru	387	39 very dark sea green	3812	188
11 very light old gold	677	886	40 medium peacock green	959	186
12 dark golden brown	975	355	41 dark violet-blue	333	119
13 medium golden brown	976	1001	42 dark violet	552	99
14 bright Christmas red	666	46	43 medium lavender	210	108
15 bright orange	608	332	44 light lavender	211	342
16 light tangerine	742	303	45 hunter green	3346	267
17 dark lemon	444	290	46 light pistachio green	368	214
18 very light topaz	727	293	47 light yellow-green	3348	264
19 very dark dusty rose	150	59	48 very dark emerald green	3818	923
20 cranberry	603	62	49 dark emerald green	910	230
21 very light dusty rose	151	73	50 Kelly green	702	226
22 light carnation	893	27	51 bright chartreuse	704	256
23 very light carnation	894	26	52 very dark blue-green	500	683
24 very light salmon	3713	1020	53 dark celadon green	3815	877
25 salmon	760	1022	54 light blue-green	503	876
26 very light terra cotta	3779	868	55 dark Christmas red	498	1005
27 very light peach flesh	948	1011	56 pale pumpkin	3825	323
28 medium dark navy blue	336	150	57 light copper	922	1003
29 very dark blue	824	164	58 dark garnet	814	45

Web resources

Index

Credits

All illustrations and photographs are the copyright of Quarto Publishing plc. While every effort has been made to credit contributors, Quarto would like to apologize should there have been any omissions or errors—and would be pleased to make the appropriate correction for future editions of the book.

READING A CHART

A cross stitch design is worked from a chart onto evenweave fabric by counting the blocks or threads in the fabric to position the stitches accurately. Each cross stitch is represented in this book by a colored cross occupying one block of fabric. Unfilled fabric blocks on a motif, letter, or border show the number of unworked blocks that separate groups of stitches. As a general rule, start stitching at the center of a cross stitch design, working outward from the center of the chart by working one complete cross stitch for every colored cross shown on the chart.

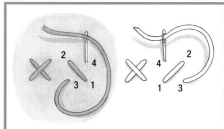

FORMING THE STITCHES Each cross can be formed exactly as shown above left, or the top and bottom diagonal stitches can be worked to slant in the opposite direction as shown above right. Whichever way you prefer to stitch, remember to be consistent, making sure the top diagonals of each cross slant in the same direction.

CATEGORY The motifs are divided into 11 different themes.

STITCH COLOR KEY A key runs across the top of each page and indicates which thread color should be used to stitch each cross shown on the chart. Fifty-eight colors are used throughout the book and each color is cross-referenced to both DMC and Anchor floss color numbers on pages 254.

NUMBERS Each motif is numbered and cross-referenced to the list of motif sizes at the back of the book.

BACKGROUND GRID To make counting easier, the background grid on each page is divided by thin black lines into blocks of five squares by five.

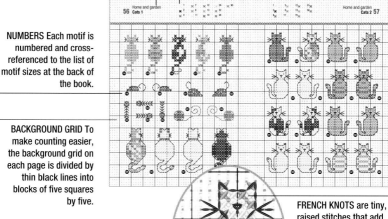

BACKSTITCH LINES are used to outline and define areas of cross stitch and these are shown as straight stitches on the charts.

FRENCH KNOTS are tiny, raised stitches that add detail and are often used to depict an eye on a bird or animal. They are shown on the charts as tiny solid dots.

Fold out this flap to find an at-a-glance guide explaining how to use the charts in this book